Mirror Images

Joc de miralls

Catalan Studies

Translations and Criticism

Josep M. Solà-Solé
General Editor

Vol. 9

PETER LANG
New York • San Francisco • Bern • Baltimore
Frankfurt am Main • Berlin • Wien • Paris

Carme Riera

Mirror Images

Joc de miralls

Translated from Catalan by
Cristina de la Torre

Published with the cooperation of the
Institució de les Lletres Catalanes

PETER LANG
New York • San Francisco • Bern • Baltimore
Frankfurt am Main • Berlin • Wien • Paris

Library of Congress Cataloging-in-Publication Data

Riera, Carme.
  [Joc de miralls. English]
  Mirror images: Carme Riera's Joc de miralls / translated by Cristina de la Torre.
    p.   cm. — (Catalan studies; vol. 9)
  I. Title. II. Series.
  PC3942.28.I37J6313   1993   849'.9354—dc20   93-9535
  ISBN 0-8204-2077-8   CIP
  ISSN 1058-1642

Die Deutsche Bibliothek-CIP-Einheitsaufnahme

Riera, Carme:
Mirror images: Carme Riera's Joc de miralls /Cristina de la Torre. - New York;
Bern; Berlin; Frankfurt/M.; Paris; Wien: Lang, 1993
  (Catalan studies; Vol. 9)
  Einheitssacht.: Joc de Miralls <engl.>
  ISBN 0-8204-2077-8
NE: GT

Cover design by James F. Brisson.

The paper in this book meets the guidelines for permanence and durability of
the Committee on Production Guidelines for Book Longevity of the
Council on Library Resources.

© Peter Lang Publishing, Inc., New York 1993

Printed in the United States of America.

Based on both the original Catalan (*Joc de miralls,* 1989; Ramón Llull Prize for Novel, Spain) and (*Por persona interpuesta,* 1989) the author's own Spanish version of the novel.

This translation has been funded with the generous help of *La Dirrección General del Libro y Bibliotecas del Ministerio de Cultura de España.*

ACKNOWLEDGEMENTS

I would like to thank everyone who played a part in this project. Concha Alborg gave me *Joc de miralls*. Susan Kirkpatrick first mentioned the possibility of translating it. The staff of Peter Lang was supportive all along, especially my editor Michael Flamini. The assistance of Alice Hickcox, of the Emory University Faculty Information and Technology Center, proved essential with the final preparation of the manuscript. As ever, Erdmann Waniek gave generously of his time, expert eye, and good cheer. I am also particularly indebted to Carme Riera for her gracious hospitality and her openness to discussion.

The Emory University Research Committee and the Ministry of Culture of Spain provided summer grants which greatly facilitated my work.

For Luisa Cotoner

Do not trouble yourself wondering whether your relations with the goddess Cytherea will sour. On the contrary, every day you will have more possibilities of being loved, truly loved. I will love you always. But, since I have no right to claim you, when you tell me that you have found Bettina Brentano I will just reply that she did not see Goethe's white hair but rather "the halo of the immortals."

Emilia Pardo Bazán in a letter
to Benito Pérez Galdós

PART I

Bettina Brentano has been waiting a long time for this encounter. To be here she has traveled disguised as a man in a decrepit carriage on thief-infested roads, still icy even though it is already spring. She has pleaded with Wieland, Goethe's secretary, and has disarmingly offered him her virginity as a reward. On this, the appointed day, she wears a blue silk dress provocatively gathered at the breast with satin ribbons, which then falls freely in abundant pleats perhaps ashamed of such clear daring. The brown curls do not frame her face as usual; today they are held back with an aquamarine beret in a way that makes her look less like a child.

Before leaving home she rehearsed a repertory of smiles and greetings, but now her lips refuse to part. She is overcome by feelings of insecurity. Perhaps her skirt is wrinkled or her hair out of place. If at least she had a mirror! It would be best to leave or, better still, not to have come at all. She should have postponed it altogether. If she only could, if it were not improper for a well-bred young lady, she would escape swiftly down the stairs. Bettina wishes she could be far, very far away, but is unable to move. Her legs are heavy as tree trunks, rooted to the floor like Daphne's.

When the door opens she feels her throat in the grip of a frigid hand while her cheeks are aflame. She looks away toward the console. In a Sèvres vase she recognizes a delicate miniature depiction of Diana, the huntress, giving chase to a deer by a creek. Only when Goethe is next to her, is she able to look at him for the first time.

I am obsessed with Bettina Brentano, whose image has been superimposed on my own memories these last few hours. It is as if only by evoking her, by trying to fathom her feelings, I can put some order into mine. I have waited just as long to meet Corbalán as she did to come face to face with Goethe. Fortunately I did not have to travel the distance that separates Kassel from Weimar, or shoot at the ghosts that populate the forest night, or sleep in the open at the foot of the city walls of Magdeburg. Unlike someone taking part in initiation rites, I was also spared from solving enigmas and overcoming deadly lures to prepare for the great encounter; I did not even need to compromise my virtue to the secretary in order to reach more quickly the seraphic vision, the Olympian sight of the master that would leave me mute and in tears. A matter of tradition? Perhaps. I am aware of the enormous importance that Corbalán has for me, of the prestige of this mysterious figure that, in my opinion, far surpasses any other Latin American writer.

I am, indeed, much better off than Bettina: I shall not have to lie like her if I should see him again. If I manage to get the interview I shall not have to pretend that I want to write his biography simply to flatter him, as she did. I realize that my relation with Corbalán seems prefigured in, and inevitably burdened by, Brentano's with Goethe. Is this a purely metonymic trick to help me write? Could be. Nevertheless, the fact remains that Corbalán is deeply interested in Goethe's work. Still, I dislike Bettina. Her behavior seems to me that of a spoiled flirt dazzled by prestige; I would not want it to influence me. More than anything in the world I want to be Corbalán's friend. So, to make a good first impression, I put on a very flattering blue dress and even some make-up. I wanted him to look at me a little longer than at all the other people who were there to welcome him. I think I was successful, even though he did not recognize me. My name did not ring any bells. Later, after I reminded him that we had corresponded for a while, he nodded vaguely. He appeared to be straining to locate, in a remote corner of his faltering memory, a single feature, the smallest trait that could provide a clue for a possible identification. I, however, had expected to be readily remembered and gladly encountered, even if only out of vanity on his part, given the half dozen extremely cordial and highly encouraging letters he had sent me, that never gave the impression of being mere formalities or following the standard model for answering letters from admirers. He did smile at me very openly, it is true, and thanked me for coming to welcome him. But that was all. In the end, could I truly have hoped for any special signs of affection? We wrote for a year while I was a freshman in college, a period that is distinctly etched into my mind. Two of my letters went unanswered and another was returned marked «Addressee unknown». Sometime later I read in the newspapers that Corbalán had decided to leave Europe and go back to his country to fight the dictatorship.

I have to admit that he impressed me even more than I had expected, although I could not pinpoint the source of his charisma nor explain what makes him so attractive. But it has little to do with his ability to create fictitious worlds or with his status as a hero, survivor of torture and jail. It is the man himself, not the myth nor the author, who holds me spellbound. It could be that I know the writer so well that he seems like an old friend with whom I have shared so much: hours poring over his work, taking the pieces apart, playing along with and observing his tactics, even correcting him at times. I do know him well. Corbalán the man, though, eludes me. I cannot quite figure out the secret of his magnetism, his power of seduction. It is not his body, elegant if a bit too languid and excessively thin, which carries the stigma of cuts and burns; nor is it his serious, almost somber air which seems to hide a certain never-conquered shyness despite having played the role of cosmopolitan celebrity used to rubbing elbows with politicians and high-powered bankers, and with ladies who speak three languages at once while sipping colorful drinks. It is also not his piercing eyes or the sensual mouth, nor his way of looking and moving his lips. It might be his hair. The exuberantly lush mane remarkable for someone his age; the salt-and-pepper strands tousled as if by ancient winds, gusts distant and romantic, rising from the pages of *Werther* or from the lonely deserts of the pampas. "Maybe my hair will shock you," he joked. "These are locks befitting a world-class genius, a scalp that would have made the day of any Sioux Indian... While in jail I pondered the possibility of escaping using my hair as a rope... I assure you that Melissande would be jealous and frightened of me! And God knows if Pelleas..."

He politely refused all interviews, shielding himself behind the wearying trip and his fragile health, "a heart delicate as the sigh of a nun, encased in a body too clumsy to treat it the way it deserves." And he declined to hold a press conference.

"Please, I beg you to excuse me. I am exhausted. I don't like to fly... planes make me claustrophobic. I hate enclosed spaces, probably because I'm still not used to being free... My emotions overwhelm me and that is not good in my condition. I need to rest now. In three days I have to attend the Peace Conference in Madrid. I am rewriting my speech. I want to speak with clarity and verve. As soon as I'm finished with that we can talk, if you wish. Please get in touch with my publisher, ask for Celia who is so kind... Right, Celia? Here, you know her already, the best public relations agent anywhere on earth..."

At this point he smilingly introduced a slender young woman. Then he took the arm of a dark girl, who had stayed in the background until that moment, and left. Behind him, carrying the luggage, walked a very tanned and brawny man.

The journalists gathered around Celia, a well-trained corporate creature who seemed familiar to me in spite of the fact that I do not habitually attend gatherings of the publishing trade. I felt thoroughly stupid about my shyness. And then, just like Bettina, I desperately wanted to cry, but out of anger rather than exhilaration, afraid that I let slip the only opportunity to set up a meeting with Corbalán. Celia most likely won't bother with a request from me. She will probably just play helpless since the private interview I want does not entail any kind of publicity or profit. I'm such an idiot, I'll never learn. I did not even mention the fact that I'm writing my thesis about his work and that it is essential that I discuss it with him.

I make my way across the enormous hall, through a throng of Scandinavian pensioners less awful than one might expect. They even excuse themselves and step aside, while overhead dull metallic voices announce the various flights. Actually the airport is not all that crowded, considering that it is so early in September. At the exit door I catch a glimpse of Corbalán getting into a brown CX with a Barcelona license plate. I make a split second decision: hail a taxi and tell the driver to follow that car.

An uneven light hovers over the grass. I am grateful for the fact that Corbalán arrived at this time of year and not before when the city's outline was dirtied by the summer haze, when the low sky, taut as a pregnant belly, appeared buttressed by TV antennas. This evening the air is clear and the setting sun softly turns off the last rays of daylight, cloaking the sour silhouettes of factories and crumbling warehouses that line the expressway to Castelldefels.

Luckily the CX takes the Ronda loop to avoid downtown. I shock myself: I would never have guessed that I would play the part of stealthy escort to Corbalán on his first stopover in Barcelona. Images of Pablo flood my senses. There's something decadently cosmopolitan and at once Bohemian about him—echoes of champagne and revelry in a storybook castle that a marquis, with tuxedo and monocle, pretends to give to his current flame. He has a hint of revolutionary alienation—flashes of film clips like the edgy and visionary Christ, followed by a swarm of beggars, that Pasolini conjured up—which becomes tangible thanks to his mane. And beyond his mane all of its easy associations: hermits tempted by shameless courtesans, cardboard Samsons, savage Amazonian tribes. But there is something more subtle, indecipherable. The voice? The gestures? The way of looking? No. Maybe intimations of an imminent disaster (the plane just lost its right wing), a view from a precipice (the train gets derailed while crossing a bridge), a door opening onto the void (a monstrous, all-devouring mouth). My steps are guided by a magnetic force. The force of desire. The force born of the desire to know. But perhaps it is nothing but a series of masks. Appearances, trompe l'œil, make-up, prostheses. Exorcisms, rites. The irresistible allure of that ephemeral apparition which camouflages the dark call of the shadows, the magma of the night.

The street lamps flicker on suddenly as we turn into Diagonal Boulevard. I am delighted to be on this wide and stately tree-lined avenue that presents a more gratifying image of Barcelona.

"Are you getting off here, too?" inquires the taxi driver when the CX stops before the Princesa Sofía Hotel.

I start for the lobby. The dark-skinned, burly young man tries to block my way.

"I'm sorry but Señor Corbalán does not wish to be disturbed and he does not grant interviews."

As though those words were not addressed to me I ignore them and attempt to go past him.

"Excuse me, Señorita, perhaps you didn't hear me. Señor Corbalán will not see you. So, please, leave."

In spite of his designer clothes and the mellowness of his South American accent, one can still detect undertones of the tough neighborhood bully.

"Oh, what a delightful coincidence. I love Corbalán's work and it would be wonderful to talk with him... I didn't know he was staying here. Thank you for the information... You see, I'm coming to see the manager, I'm his niece."

Before the doorman's at once astonished and mocking gaze the young man dissolves into all sorts of apologies. "Actually, I was just following orders. The writer is in very poor health and journalists can be so persistent... such pests,

really... Maybe tomorrow, if Don Pablo is feeling better..."
He himself will gladly inquire if a meeting is possible. "Call
me around ten, or rather let me have your number. I'll see
what I can do."

I have no choice but to step into the hotel. I have never
before set foot in the Princesa Sofía. Without the least hesitation, I go on ahead as if I were perfectly accustomed to its
padded and vulgar luxury.

13 September 1978

Wieland, Goethe's secretary, cuts a rather caricaturesque figure. He is wearing a faded robe that reaches down to his feet, and a pair of threadbare slippers. He works in a dark and disorderly room. The chairs are piled high with clothes and papers; stacks of books cover the table and spill onto the floor. Wieland does not know Bettina. He has no idea of who she is or what she wants at this scandalous hour, at nap time, this girl who feigns shyness to charm the old poet, who lies freely about a former acquaintance between them, back when she still wore her luscious hair down and had never yet danced at any balls.

"Yes, it could be that we met, but I cannot recall. Forgive me, I am very old."

"Just try to imagine me three years ago and it will be as good as remembering me... And, since we're old friends, could you introduce me to Goethe?"

"Hello. We spoke yesterday at the hotel, remember? You asked me to call about seeing Don Pablo."

"What newspaper do you work for?"

"None, actually. The questions I want to ask are for my own benefit. I admire Corbalán's work and am doing research on it. Occasionally I write a piece for *Imago*, the magazine. Do you know it? I think it is sold in Itálica. Perhaps, if Corbalán doesn't object, I could publish the interview there."

"Fine. This afternoon at four, then. You will have at most two hours. All right? Naturally, before you publish anything, Don Pablo will have the right to look it over."

The telephone seemed to add force to his words. I agreed to his requests, which sounded more like orders. Still, I was lucky. Yesterday I thought he wouldn't move a muscle for my sake. He didn't even seem to like me. Could it be that he really believed that I was the manager's niece?

The gurgling of the water in the fountain keeps time to Bettina's footsteps. The shape of the first swallows is outlined against the sky, like cutouts on a piece of taffeta cloth. Bettina gathers her skirt with the left hand and slowly climbs the statue-lined staircase. Before crossing the threshold she rereads the note that Wieland just gave her:

> *Bettina Brentano, sister of Sofia, daughter of*
> *Maximiliana, granddaughter of Sofia La Roche,*
> *wishes to see you. She says she feels intimidated*
> *and that is why she asked me to write this note,*
> *as an amulet that will give her the necessary courage.*

Etchings cover the walls and the furniture is sparse. There is a red divan, some mahogany chairs also upholstered in red, and a sideboard. The room is small and has only one window that opens onto an enclosed garden.

Carrying a bouquet of roses I cross the vast lobby. More than a station in outer space or the duty-free shop at the international terminal of an airport, it resembles an outsized cosmopolitan stable for pure-bred cattle.

Corbalán sits waiting for me at the bar, almost buried between the cushions of a plush and pious armchair.

"You're the woman who wants to interview me, is that right?"

He gets up and offers his hand while looking me over from head to toe, as if calculating my height.

"What will you have to drink? It's the perfect time for a cup of coffee... Or perhaps some cognac, or a liqueur?"

He gestures sparingly, just enough to accompany his words and underline shades of meaning where his voice seems to rest.

"Are you a teetotaler by any chance? Don't. You'll never reach old age. Besides, if you teach literature it's good to know about booze. Many a writer's words are soaked in it. The list of alcoholic writers is far from short... Malcolm

Lowry, Truman Capote, Hemingway, Joyce... So many of them in the nineteenth century... Not to mention the critics, your Menéndez Pelayo, for instance... During our freshman year in college we had to read his *History of Heterodoxy*... Do you want some advice? Never distrust drinkers. Well, what can I do for you..."

I want to say that I don't like cognac and that, quite to the contrary, I'm a prime candidate for Alcoholics Anonymous, that on weekends sometimes my stomach can get alarmingly soggy... but I do not say anything. What possible interest could Corbalán have in my life?

"There's an angle to your personality that intrigues me and that, in a way, is related to a theme that you explore in your latest work: the theme of seduction. You seem to me extraordinarily attractive, perhaps in part due to the aura of mystery that surrounds you..."

"Thank you."

A laconic answer accompanied by a splendid smile that begins in his eyes and extends, wide and diffused, to lips that reveal gleaming, perfect teeth. Then silence. I insist.

"What does seduction mean to you?"

"It is my main obsession as a writer. I begin by wanting to seduce the reader so that she cannot suddenly abandon me, so that she will read me to the very end. The play with appearances, the ambiguous signs, the varied connotations that characterize my work are all aimed at bringing her to me, at making her mine, at seducing her. But at the same time that the reader is seduced, she becomes a seducer too. A seducer is someone who has been seduced."

"And personally, does Pablo Corbalán like to seduce?"

"What do you expect me to say to that? It might be more professional to answer negatively, but I would be lying. I'm already past fifty... Do you remember Aschenbach in *Death in Venice*? No, wait, don't jump to conclusions. Aschenbach, painted like a flaming fag and chasing a seraphic adolescent... It has nothing to do with beauty or creativity. No.

Great seduction tales all end in death because there's nowhere else to go. Therefore, since I'm an old man and I'm not ready to die yet, I should avoid such situations... Life is short, at least what I've left of it... But I don't do it. I'm too vulnerable, even fragile, and much too tired to disguise my helplessness, which always proves disarming."

"Maybe in your case the attraction lies in the mystery, in the secrets around you, all of which may be perfectly studied, even planned by some image consultant in a public relations firm."

"Can you really believe that? Do I truly project that impression? Wonderful! The gods are seduced by mystification, which is the basis of ritual. Baudelaire, in a fascinating text extolling the merits of make-up, reminds us that a painted woman fulfills a kind of sacred function. Make-up suppresses the body and elevates the spirit. If anyone thinks that my supposed seductiveness is the result of a meticulous process of elaboration, so much the better. What primarily attracts us is the wrapping, the cover, the symbol, much more than any deep meaning. I would even go so far as to say that what moves us about beauty is precisely its artifice, never its natural quality."

"Your words seem to imply that you favor surfaces, posturing, a frilly gift-wrap aesthetics..."

"It may sound frivolous but the surface is, in the final analysis, the deepest part. Take the skin, for instance. Can you think of anything more apparent and yet more profound?"

His fingers edge close, almost touching my arm, but the hand draws back at the last moment and rests on the leather couch where we are sitting on opposite sides of a tape recorder.

"You expressed similar thoughts in one of your essays. It was the one called «Baroque Imagery» if I'm not mistaken. You mention that poets transform the body of a woman either into precious materials, such as marble and pearls that will stand the test of time and pass from generation to generation, or into flowers condemned to wilt quickly, to live the briefest of lives. Thus, by comparison, they seek to make her immortal or ephemeral."

"The poets themselves poked fun at those two alternatives. Cervantes in *Don Quixote*, as well as in one of his exemplary novels, *Mr. Showcase, Attorney-at-Law*, joked about how any old rhyme-maker is likely to squander his treasures in the effort to capture the essence of his loved one. Quevedo observed that flesh and blood women had been turned into flowers, roses, gardens and springs. In fact, every Baroque poet grappled intensely with the problem we still face: namely, time. Time is the enemy, as Pound said. But Baroque poets were mistaken when they tried to ennoble and stylize their women by comparing them to precious stones or flowers. There is nothing so noble, so glorious, so beautiful and perfect as the skin, the eyes, the lips, the breasts or the genitals of the beloved. Nothing compares to that, condemned as it ultimately is to decay and perish. I guess that in flights of optimism the poet saw his beloved in more lasting terms and likened her to noble and durable materials. On the other hand, when he succumbed to pessimism the point of comparison was flowers, subject to imminent death and therefore exquisite."

Corbalán does not seem to be addressing me, or anyone else for that matter. He has lowered his voice and his eyes appear fixed on the carpet, or perhaps on the tips of his very polished shoes. He seems weary... There is a long silence. Pieces of other conversations, in other languages, float on the muzak and reach my ears. Then he goes on, almost in a whisper.

"I grew up in a garden. My earliest memories are all of scents. December has the aroma of jasmine which is how paradise must smell; in summertime odors always reach their peak at night... Have you ever had a whiff of freshly baked bread? And of wheat right after it's harvested?... They smell of childhood because they are joyful fragrances. As a kid I spent long periods in the countryside. My father had a big farm, Trebujar, in the north near Venusia."

There is another silence. I become aware that the conversation has taken a turn. Corbalán's memory now travels back on a private road. I sense that the writer is wandering around his own Eden in search of darkened splendors.

"Please tell me about your childhood."

"I don't like to talk about my life. And remember you assured me that this would be a strictly literary interview. In that case my memories or, for that matter, the place where I was born in 1927, are irrelevant."

"Wait a second. I always thought you were born on January 14th, 1926."

"Very good. I was just checking how well you knew my vital statistics."

"Well, I'm doing research on your work and I am supposed to know them, after all. Your father was a famous doctor, your mother was blond and beautiful and liked to play the piano... you had two brothers..."

"Two sisters. Shall we talk about literature?"

"As you wish, Señor Corbalán, but wouldn't you agree that autobiography affects the written works?"

"The man is never the author. Proust insisted that anyone could find out every detail about Racine's life, for example, but they still wouldn't be able to tell where his creative genius came from. And Proust himself, that refined and asthmatic dandy, was not the protagonist of *Remembrance of Things Past*. Certainly there are elements of one's life that get reworked with more or less accuracy... In that sense any novel is autobiographical."

"There are remarkable differences between *Relay* and *Senseless Days*, with respect to both narrative perspective and plot. There seems to be no relation between the closed, almost claustrophobic universe of *Relay* and *Senseless Days'* vast epic panorama showing the crucial role that the so-called 'silent majority' played in the fall of Luzón."

"True. *Senseless Days* could be taken as a faithful chronicle of political events in my country during a specific time, as endured by the humble, the outcast, the disenfranchised. A situation that I knew, and suffered, myself. In other words it was a novel with a purpose; it served as testimony, as denunciation. In *Relay* I was obsessed by something totally different: an individual process. This is the story of a passion that has nothing to do with me personally but that, in a way, is closely related to my intense need for introspection, for isolation. *Relay* was written in jail as the only way of coping with that agonizing situation, it was an escape, naturally an inward escape."

"In this work there is a conspicuous exploration of the possibilities of play and ambiguity, whereas in *Senseless Days* everything is clear, evident, almost bordering on the dogmatic."

"You're absolutely right. As I mentioned before, *Senseless Days* belongs to a stage of my life that is over and done. Let me be clear about one thing: I'm not repudiating it, but I feel rather detached from it, as if someone other than myself had written it. Play and games are key features of *Relay*, which is precisely why costumes and masks are so prominent. «Give me a mask and I'll tell you the truth,» wrote Oscar Wilde. In Latin 'persona' means mask. Ezra Pound also wrote some verses to that effect."

"Throughout this interview you have quoted writers such as Proust, Baudelaire... You have mentioned Pound twice. Do you feel a special affinity to him?"

"Most definitely. I'm very interested in his work. I think he is one of the best poets of the twentieth century and he has been trashed by some critics for his political convictions."

"You yourself went from being a writer who attacked the system to collaborating with the government of General

Patiño and serving as its ambassador. After Patiño's fall you returned to Itálica to fight the dictatorship and spent ten years in jail. Finally, as a result of international pressure, you have been set free. Strangely enough, your radical views seem to have mellowed. In your press conference in New York you refused to make any political statements and now you are defending Ezra Pound. Seems odd in a fighter like you."

"Not really. You agreed that Pound's poetry is remarkable, and I judge him exclusively as a poet. In political terms he made a wrong choice, but he acted in good faith nevertheless. He truly believed in Mussolini."

"Señor Corbalán, at one time you were labeled «a dangerous revolutionary» by the government of your country, isn't that right? Your words now are closer to those of a middle-class liberal."

"Well, there are many ways of fighting dictatorships, and some are misguided even in spite of their good intentions. Would you face an armed street gang all by yourself, at night, in a deserted alley? Surely you'd try to escape or hide, wouldn't you? Resisting would be absolutely suicidal. It would be tantamount to inviting a handful of thugs to rape or kill you. The same happens to a revolutionary who confronts dictatorship bare-chested, so to speak. He is at a great disadvantage. There's no denying that. No regime, even the most heinous one, deserves to have oneself martyred. It makes more than enough victims on its own. Look, a Chinese proverb sums it up quite well: «It's better to wait out the tide than to swim upstream»."

"Granted, but if everyone agreed with that nothing would ever change, there would never have been any revolutionaries, let alone revolutions. And revolutions are what propel history forward..."

"They are the locomotives, as Marx put it. Sounds perfectly nineteenth century, don't you think? Do you know why in Spain you were able to make the transition to a new order without any bloodshed? Because you waited... Having come face to face with my own death I can tell you that life is much too precious to give it up in vain. In my youth I risked my life fighting for political ideals, today I would not do it. Besides, the mission of the writer is above politics; it consists exclusively in creating works of universal value. It's men who should take political stands, not writers. That is, Corbalán the citizen, not the author. Read my speech about peace, it will probably come out in the papers. Perhaps it will clarify some points for you."

"Could you possibly summarize it briefly?"

"I will speak about peace, of course. But the details must come as a surprise. I will also reveal some facts that are essential to understand the history of Itálica. It will be very risky. The leaders of my country will not be pleased, of that I'm sure. This will be my political statement and I hope to have the strength to make it..."

"Are you afraid?"

"Yes, why not admit it. I'm afraid and full of doubts. But doubts are creative... I am no longer interested in absolute truths, I'm too old for that. Facts bore me. In that sense we should all learn from scientists, who never feel they're in possession of the one truth, whereas inquisitors, tyrants, and dictators do. They are unaware that truth does not exist, that there are only appearances, mirages. As Nietzsche proclaimed «Truth is no longer true once it has been revealed.» Revolution also does not exist, there is only the appearance of it, the abstract idea. And that idea prevails because both the capitalist and the Stalinist systems oppose it. The clearest proof that it doesn't exist is the fact that everyone is still expecting it to happen..."

The tape has stopped. I start to turn it over.

"No, please, leave it off. I guess those were the questions of the journalist, the ones for *Imago*, isn't that so? But you personally want to explore other aspects of my work... It's getting kind of late," he claims looking at his Rolex; "this is the same model that Ché Guevara was wearing when he was captured. After his death General Ovando Candía kept it. Guevara got it as a gift and so did I. I'm very tired now. Please come back tonight, around nine."

"I would like to say something... To tell you the truth, I really..."

"The truth concerns you greatly, doesn't it?"

"The truth is that I'm not the hotel manager's niece."

"I already knew that. Don't worry. I'll see you later."

All during our interview the dark brawny man sat nearby leafing through magazines.

15 September 1978

Suddenly the door opened and there stood Goethe serious and aloof. He stared at me intently. My eyes did not dare to hold his gaze. We remained like that for a few moments. Tears started rolling down my cheeks. He took me in his arms. I hid my face in his chest, next to his heart. I could hear it beating. My eyelids closed and when I opened them again I realized that I was beginning a new life.

I spent the time until nine o'clock transcribing the interview. At the reception desk the clerk indicated that Corbalán was expecting me in room 498.

I did not need to knock. Just as I was getting ready to do so the door opened. Corbalán was saying good-bye to the dark young woman with the high cheekbones who brushed past me without a glance. She returned almost immediately, claiming to have forgotten her appointment book, and this time her eyes drilled into me. She had cat-like eyes, honey-colored with green flecks similar to Corbalán's own; eyes that would be beautiful if they were not so guarded. While her eyes declared war, her lips smiled peace and she excused herself softly for the interruption. As she lingered at the end of the hallway addressing Corbalán, she scratched the air good-bye with long, scarlet-nailed fingers. "Please, don't exhaust yourself," she said to him, "I'll be back soon."

The chaos in his suite took me by surprise. Mounds of books and newspapers, empty bottles and glasses on the floor. On the bed, an open suitcase displaying a woman's undergarments. A lace bra left on the carpet like some forgotten trophy. I wondered whether to pick it up or just ignore it. Corbalán pointed me to an ugly gray armchair by a coffee-table. Susana Rinaldi's canned voice was blaring from a record player.

"Do you know Susana Rinaldi? Really! So you must like tangos too...!"

"I love them."

"Wonderful. So do I. Rinaldi is the best, after Gardel of course. Many years ago we happened to be in Tucumán at the same time. In that sense I have been luckier than Cortázar who wrote her a poem:

I never laid eyes on you,
but yours are the records
that furnish this Paris apartment
where fake mirrors have you Piafing on corners."

He pulls out an album with Rinaldi on the cover. The angle of the photograph highlights her face and hands against a black background. "I saw it this morning, in a store near the hotel. I couldn't resist the temptation of buying it. I'd like you to take it, it would just break in my suitcase. Play it sometime when you think of me. Shall we continue with the interview? I would very much like to read some of what you've written about my work."

I promise to drop off some manuscripts at the reception desk the very next morning. I start the tape recorder and mention the ever changing point of view in *Relay*, the constant use of mirrors which multiply the angles of vision and trap us in a tangle of false reflections. I ask about literary influences: Borges, Mujica, Sábato, Pose (about whom he does not wish to comment). I bring up the unmentionables, Luengo and García Ortega. He elaborates on the technical aspects of *Relay*, the different linguistic registers, how as the masks fill the ballrooms (which serve as chapters of the novel) the din grows to resemble a symphony and dwindles to whispers towards the end, when the curtain is about to fall. We talk about Mario's claustrophobic obsession, his metamorphoses, about the role of music.

Corbalán's comments will be very valuable, I'm convinced, but at the moment I feel incapable of pressing the play button and listening to his voice next to mine, to our voices saved together on that tape that I stare at and put away, reserving the pleasure for some time in the future. It is stored among my notes, some chapters of my thesis which I will summarize tonight so that Corbalán can take them to Madrid. Or, maybe, I will hand-deliver them myself at Barajas Airport. Meeting his plane in Madrid would no doubt be the ultimate whimsy of this summer. I really would just love to greet him again, to follow him by taxi to his hotel: the Ritz, the Palace, perhaps the Eurobuilding? He will surely have a suite, hopefully cozier than the one I left an hour ago expelled by a bodyguard named Oscar, and by Sara the secretary.

"You've been very fortunate. Don Pablo never grants interviews. You should be grateful to Oscar and to your uncle, the manager," she comments, and her lips flash me a smile that belie the lightning in her eyes, as she flutters like a blinded moth around Corbalán. Caught off-guard, I am unable to come up with an ironic reply and just make a hasty exit.

I stay up the whole night polishing my best pages on *Relay*, the novel that he prefers and about which we have talked more extensively, even though my thesis deals mainly with *Senseless Days*. I reread the chapters once they are finished and find them utterly banal. I pull out his letters, handwritten in meticulous script so different from his handwriting now, vacillating and tortured. During the first interview I did not notice the slight tremor of his hands, very much in evidence when he writes, especially in the way he secures the paper with the pen and pushes it with his fingers. His handwriting is angular, elongated like crane legs, those same cranes that, he reminded me, asked Hèrmes-Mercury to make up the alphabet.

We talked more about his childhood, about the house where he spent his summers, and as farewell he dedicated *Relay* with a sort of invitation: «For Teresa, hoping that she will reclaim a wall covered with wisteria and words for her old friend Corbalán.» The one for *Senseless Days* is a lot more cryptic: «Imagine a moment, new over time, consisting of remembrances bare and light and numinous.» It was a very warm exchange, much more intimate than our first. This was the Corbalán that I had gleaned from the letters that he wishes to reread now, even though they belong to a period that is almost lost to him. Call me Pablo, he asked just before we parted.

All of a sudden the notoriously reserved Goethe, who shuns love, who habitually flees from entanglements, who has never wished to run those kinds of risks, seems to realize that Bettina Brentano could well be more than just an ordinary admirer. At least she is unlike all the others because she embraces him with utter abandon, and taking one of his hands in hers guides it under her camisole to her left breast. She wishes for Goethe's hand to remember after she has gone the feel of her young skin, the sweet shape of her adolescent body as if this contact will be capable of evoking desire or, at the very least, a memory or a poem.

Yes, I talked with him about Bettina. I told him that I have put into writing everything about our meetings because I don't want to forget the slightest detail, and that Bettina and Goethe serve as a parallel.

"I don't mean to disappoint you," he said, "but neither in *Poetry and Truth,* nor in the conversations that Eckermann so faithfully transcribed, does Goethe ever mention Bettina by name. Perhaps there are sentences that could be construed as referring to her, for example when he points out that some German women write very well... Are you familiar with their correspondence? I find Bettina's infinitely more beautiful. Even though her letters are very literary, that is fictitious, they are much more sincere, far more authentic than Goethe's who always answered in a courteous and mechanical manner... On the other hand, the letters that Beethoven wrote to Brentano are truly wonderful. Beethoven was utterly taken with Bettina:

My friend, you came at a sad moment when I was overcome by despair. But your presence worked a miracle, it was enough to bring me back to life again. Since you left I have been terribly unsettled, restless, and unable to work. I walked along the alley at Schönbrunn and there were no angels to comfort me the way only you know how, my angel.

Did you know that one? It's not all that great. Andrei Hevesy includes it in Beethoven's biography, a book I read during my student days, published by the Iberoamerican Publishing Company where I once worked."

I am happy and set to go to Madrid even if it means putting up with the frowns of his companions. I care about Pablo. I have waited for him for a very long time and now I am willing to run the risk of making him angry or, worse, having him say he does not know me. I'm going to type out a summary of my notes on *Relay* and this very night, as if it were an urgent love letter that cannot wait to be sent through normal channels, I will take it myself to the hotel concierge to be hand-delivered to Don Pablo Corbalán.

15 and 16 September 1978

You will never know that I was in Madrid to welcome you once more. It was only after waiting all morning at the airport that I happened, while in the ladies' room, to over-hear the news on the radio. The announcer's voice hit me like a closed fist in the stomach: "Italican writer Pablo Corbalán was found dead in a hotel room in Barcelona." I fainted and had to be rushed to the airport infirmary. I fol-lowed you—or at least that's what I thought I was doing—for no other reason than the pleasure of seeing you, of being with you. I had no desires other than to accompany you for as long as you, or they, wished; now they, too, have van-ished without a trace. I do not even have the solace of your letters which are in the hands of the judge, or of the tape with the first interview, which the police requisitioned. I do not dare to listen to the last one. No one knows that I have it. I cannot get used to your absence. It has left an aching void in me. I dreamed that I was waiting for you in a misty sta-tion, out in the open, under a dense and noisy rain that soaked everything. Your train did not arrive. I waited in the same spot for a long time, probably months. I know because the passengers of the first trains were dressed in light sum-mer clothes and later they wore thick fur coats and com-plained about the cold. I woke up shivering.

The police don't think it was suicide. I don't know if I am on the list of suspects but they have interrogated me twice. "A lie is never a good start and you claimed to be the hotel manager's niece. He told us himself. Señor Corbalán's secre-tary inquired about it."

My fingerprints are all over the room alongside yours. Was Sara your lover? What was the meaning of her suitcase left open on top of your bed, and of that bra lying about like a trophy? I have no doubt they did away with you on orders from the government of your country. You see, neutrality did not do you any good, they riddled your stomach with pills like bullets pumping you full of barbiturates. It was not your idea, I'm convinced of that. Your death was not a suicide. You did not want to die, you told me as much. You wanted to live at any cost.

"Please explain again your relation with Corbalán."

"I admired him. I do research on his work. That is all."

"Are you positive? Then what were you doing in his room so late at night?"

"..."

I did not go in, Pablo, I didn't even knock. I slid an envelope with some typewritten pages under your door. Did you ever see them, did you get to read them?

The police claim that the envelope was not in your room when they got there.

I wonder what Bettina Brentano would have done in these circumstances.

24 September 1978

I never could have imagined that in the eyes of the press I would become the keeper of Pablo Corbalán's last will. Since the interview was published I have appeared in five newspapers and have participated in three radio programs on Latin American literature. On top of that TV crews from *Three Hundred Million* showed up yesterday. They traveled all the way from Madrid to film some footage in my home. I really regret having agreed to it. Millions of people will wander through my apartment scrutinizing my furniture, my surroundings. And what's worse, they will read the dedications that Corbalán wrote for me. I should have declined.

The interviewer was Italican but, of course, "in good standing" with the powers that be. He admitted, without the slightest trace of embarrassment, that he had never read Corbalán who actually was much better known abroad than at home.

"People have short memories. *Senseless Days* was a best-seller too long ago. Corbalán spent most of his life outside of Itálica and then in jail... The government gave its approval for the program but still, please be discreet."

I was, perhaps even too much.

"Politically I found Corbalán very moderate. However, the speech that he was about to deliver included some important revelations. That is probably why he was murdered."

"Cut!," yelled the interviewer enraged.

"I asked you to be discreet. Don't mention murder, it hasn't been proven yet. And skip the speech too. Nothing to do with politics, please. *Three Hundred Million* is a variety program: culture, leisure, that sort of thing... We are basically interested in the human side of Corbalán."

Montero went through his introduction once more without changing any of the trivia.

"Good evening. This is Pedro Montero, Italian National Television. Greetings from Barcelona where we have come to remember one of our great writers, a truly universal Italican. It was here, in this beautiful city, that Pablo Corbalán died. We will be talking with Teresa Mascaró, the young journalist who was the last to interview him. Tell us, Señorita Mascaró, what was Don Pablo like?"

"Excuse me, but I'm not a journalist..."

Montero was literally climbing the walls.

"Just answer my questions and cut out the lectures, will you? I don't care what you are or are not. And anyway, if you interviewed him it was as a journalist and not as an agent of the KGB, I presume."

I began to talk about Corbalán's magnetism, his aura of mystery, the revolutionary's mane, and he cut in.

"Like Einstein, he had the hair of a wise man. And a very handsome one, too. And now tell us, what do you think of his books?"

"They are wonderful. *Senseless Days* is a splendid chronicle of injustice and alienation. *Relay* belongs to an entirely different stage in which the search for personal identity is the main focus."

"Did you find him attractive? Rumor has it that he was quite a ladies' man..."

"I found him very polite and helpful. He had a very strong personality."

"We thank you on behalf of our audience."

As soon as they left I called Celia. She and her damned publishing house are to blame for this set-up. She pacified me by saying that the producer is a friend of hers, that she will see to it that the interview is not aired without my approval... "Besides, I'm sure you'll look ravishing," she added teasingly, "and not everyone has the chance to appear before three hundred million people to talk about Pablo Corbalán."

17 October 1978

I finally dared to play the tape but, instead of our final conversation, there was a recording of Susana Rinaldi. Thirteen songs in all, between tangos and milongas: *No One Like You, Once More, Dreaming of Barrilete, Forget Me, When You Come Back, Downhill, Another Woman, Remember Me, Barrio, For Catullo Castillo, Morocha, To My Fellowman, You Will Never Return*... None of these songs are on the record that he gave me. Even though they're all beautiful I'm crushed with disappointment. I must have put the wrong tape in my bag, but I can't understand how I could've made such a silly mistake. Maybe it was them, Oscar or Sara, who switched the tapes. Or perhaps even Corbalán himself was playing a prank on me... But why? Was he annoyed by my admiration, or by the fact that I compared myself to Bettina Brentano? Did he regret his statements, or was it his companions who found them objectionable? We were all by ourselves during the interview, at least so far as I knew...

Celia insists that Sara and Oscar are not the murderers. She's certain that they were kidnapped before Pablo was poisoned. In her opinion both were very good people and absolutely devoted to Corbalán.

24 October 1978

I went to see my parents. I wanted to explain to them in person what has been happening. They would've found out sooner or later anyway, even though they hardly ever read the newspapers. Deep down I envy them. They are oblivious to anything and everything outside the house, yet they seem happy. At times I even think it was a mistake to move out. They scolded me, as usual, because I never go back with enough time to spend at least a few days. My problems with the police did not really appear to affect them terribly much.

"So long as you're innocent, you have nothing to worry about. Poor fellow! Be very careful with what you eat, dear. Maybe it was botulism. Remember all the people who were poisoned with that batch of bad cooking oil? Most of the things that city people eat are spoiled, anyway."

Their blind faith in justice is most refreshing, given the times. Mother recalled all the accidental poisonings that she had ever heard about, and Dad wanted to know where Corbalán had been buried.

"So they just stuck him in a rented niche in Cerdanyola! How can that be? I would've thought that the government of his country would've paid to have his body flown back, if he is as important as you make him out to be."

In the afternoon we went for a walk. It was autumn already in the woods. Fallen leaves crumbled under our feet and hunters' shots could be heard in the distance. Everything seems to grow smaller and fainter, like the light. Everything except for the rush of colors exploding on the branches: browns, golds, yellows, reds, vermilions... This is the most beautiful time of year, a smooth transition between extremes. Autumn bids a gentle farewell to the luminous violence of summer and welcomes the first winter storms.

I shall make a point of enjoying everything twice, once for myself and once for Pablo.

2 November 1978

He died two months ago today. *Relay* is number one on the bestsellers list. The Peace Conference ends tomorrow and no one will have heard, or even read, the smallest fragment of Corbalán's speech. The missing bodyguard, speaking on Pablo's behalf, had refused to give any hints about it to the press to avoid having them piece it together before it was given. Besides, he argued, Don Pablo always made changes all the way up to the last minute.

During that second interview when we were alone, if we were alone, he showed me some typed pages and said that they contained crucial information. I did not have time to read through them, but perhaps this information was the reason for his death. I haven't ceased to wonder during these two months why I, usually not the assertive type, dared to follow Corbalán to his hotel and fake my identity. Over and over I have come to the conclusion that it happened that way simply because it had to. My life, just like everybody else's, is guided by the hands of fate; somewhere it was written that I would be the last person to interview Don Pablo.

Yesterday I got a call from his publisher. They want me to write an introduction and be the editor of the paperback issue of *Relay*. I am thrilled by the possibility. I discussed it with Celia at length this morning. When I first met her at the airport she seemed like a boor and I didn't like her at all. Later, when she called to negotiate buying the rights to the interview, she was a lot friendlier. Today she was downright charming. She said that the pay is not bad and that, if they like what I write, there's a good chance that they'll also ask me to edit the essays.

Since Pablo's death, *Relay* has sold 25 000 copies in Spain alone. It is still not available in Itálica, where the Ministry of Culture appears interested in doing a special edition. This is perfectly appalling: the same government that held him prisoner for ten years and that, I'm positive, had him murdered, now plans to appropriate him and turn him into a national asset. Celia insists that the political situation has improved since Cardona offered to hold elections. With or without official sanction the publisher is preparing a volume in homage to Corbalán and needs an editor. I agreed to do it.

No doubt, today has been a good day. Suárez, the police commissioner, cleared me of suspicions. "I always thought you were innocent, but a good policeman should never discard one single lead," he said as he offered me a cigarette. They were Cuban Coronas, probably the booty of a raid.

"The Corbalán case is far more complex than people imagine, and much more sinister. This is not the first time that Latin American dictators have bothersome political refugees killed. There have been at least a dozen such cases in Spain, and they've never been solved. We'll be luckier with Corbalán, you'll see," he said as farewell, "among other things because I'm in charge."

17 November 1978

Celia called this morning. She asked me to come right over. She wanted to speak to me about an urgent matter. She gave no indication of what it might be. Something of great interest to you, you'll see. Just hurry.

"How would you like to go to Itálica?" she blurted out. "I should be the one going but I can suggest that you take my place. You'd be responsible for presenting and promoting *Relay*. All expenses paid, daily allowance, plus salary."

I am happy. Almost happy.

Also, since the trip almost coincides with Christmas vacation, there won't be any need to get a substitute instructor for my classes. I'll make up the lost sessions and give exams when I get back. I'm off to Itálica!

The neighbor just asked me to turn down the music. "I'm fed up with your tangos," she yelled.

I'm going to Itálica.

I shall write your name—our names—Pablo, on a wall covered with wisteria blossoms.

20 November 1978

PART II

Calipso, 12 December 1978

Dear Celia: I'll never be able to thank you enough for having made this trip possible for me. Without your help I wouldn't have been able to come before the summer, and then it would have taken all my savings! You know better than anyone how important it is for me to get to know the setting of Corbalán's novels, to actually set foot in his country, to visit the city where he was born, the places he went to as a young man, and especially to meet the people who knew him. You're probably thinking that I'm behaving with the naiveté of a groupie. Writers don't usually inspire ardent devotion the way singers or actors do. I don't at all mind being the exception; in fact, I rather like being labeled as his "fan".

I've been here three days and I still haven't seen much of the city, aside from the airport where I had to wait four hours until my luggage showed up, the hotel, and the publishing house. I stayed busy preparing the presentation of *Relay* and it paid off. Every newspaper and all the radio and TV stations, even the most pro-government ones, mentioned the event and two thousand people came yesterday. The ballroom of the Itálica Palace was jammed. I confess I was jittery, apprehensive that at any moment the police might show up and ask us to leave. Apparently it was not too difficult to get the permissions needed for such a gathering, which seems altogether incongruous. As dense as these people must be, they might have guessed that the presentation of *Relay* was not merely a literary or even a social occasion but a political act against the government. It took me back to the late sixties, to our own rallies in homage to Machado or García Lorca. Naturally statements were read. One of them was particularly chilling: Itálica, which as you know is only one third the size and much less populated than Argentina, has at the moment two hundred thousand *desaparecidos*. The number is staggering. I can imagine that for the families and friends of these people, any good words from us "civilized Europeans" must seem insulting, like rubbing salt into an open wound. Things look very different from here, and now I clearly understand what you meant when you said that most of the time neutrality is a crime. That's why I think the presentation of *Relay* was highly significant in two respects. In the first place, because Corbalán's name was spoken proudly, even though there is little doubt that he was assassinated by the regime's secret agents, as was publicly hinted at yesterday. Secondly, because his name is becoming a rallying point for a group of young writers, artists, and intellectuals—the few that have not been jailed or sent into exile yet—who are ready to do whatever is required to regain their freedom.

Just so you can have an idea of the impact of this event, let me mention that the representative of Amnesty International was there, as was Rodríguez Ventura, who shared the Nobel Peace Prize with Pérez Esquivel. At the moment Rodríguez Ventura is the charismatic leader of the opposition and, curiously enough, the government is leaving him alone. I would've liked a chance to talk with him but it was impossible to even come near because of the mob. I did, however, get his phone number. Perhaps he is the best person to present *Relay* in Venusia next week. I'll discuss it with the Marcusi agent. By the way, I got Rodríguez Ventura's phone number from a man named Isidoro Quiñonero, an old friend of Corbalán's. He was very close to Don Pablo in his youth and is quite delightful himself. I'm having dinner at his house tomorrow and will tell you all about it in my next letter. Quiñonero is a big fan of *Senseless Days* but not of *Relay*, which he finds flawed and shallow.

Thanks for the telex, Celia. Your timing was great: I needed some cheering up right then. I gather all's well in

Barcelona and that the higher-ups are pleased. The Marcusi man congratulated me on the success of the presentation.
Warm regards,

Teresa

Calipso, 15 December 1978

Dear Celia: Calipso is beautiful, hypnotically so. I don't know of any other city more aptly named. I can't decide what enchants me more: the golden serenity of the old town with its graceful columns reminiscent of Greek temples, or the working-class sections of the city mottled with cheap houses and brightly colored tin shacks. I feel right at home in both, even though they are so vastly different. Perhaps that's the reason why it's so difficult to choose. At times the eerie stillness that pervades the old town can get on my nerves; but then, that's the main source of its dignity. The allure of the outskirts, however, is just the opposite. They are teeming with life of every sort. It's a veritable tangle of humans and animals, a mixture that can sometimes be primitive, even cruel; poverty usually suffers little shame. The area I like the least is the new city that spreads out from the left bank of the river. It is relatively modern, by now shabbily so, since it was built mostly during the prosperous fifties, when wheat exports made Itálica the economic equal of Argentina. Altogether, I think I'd keep to the contrasting Calipsos that I first mentioned. On Mondays, Wednesdays, and Fridays, I would mingle with the noisy, variegated crowds of workers in the suburbs surrounding the city, and endure the inevitable bad conscience that such places always stir up. The rest of the week, I'd seek my balance in the old quarters. I imagine it was a desire for harmony that prompted Calipso's founder, Anastasio Pantaleón de Ribera, to hire a Florentine architect and master of the Palladian style to design the patrician part of the city around the end of the XVIth century. The classic taste of Don Anastasio, who was born in Montaña of a noble family, is very gratifying even today. He is responsible for making Calipso a rare jewel in this part of the world, a Periclean Athens transplanted to the pampas. The legendary conqueror of Calipso was obsessed with antiquity to such an extent that he demanded that his Indian lovers, with whom he had innumerable descendants, call him Alexander, Achilles, Ulysses, or Patroclus. He gave cities and institutions names adapted from Greek mythology: Calipso, Venusia (not from Venice but from Venus!), Selene, Nereidas, Cianes, Andromeda. These names are still in use, mixed now with the likes of Santa Cecilia, Granada, Tituajaya, Ganapú, Xiqué. Notice that the names chosen by Pantaleón de Ribera are all feminine, belonging to goddesses, nymphs, or heroines who possessed few of the warring virtues that enflamed the conqueror. I'm just fascinated by this strange and puzzling character, so this morning I went to a small museum where a lot of his personal objects are kept: his saddle and suit of armor, some letters from Philip II, and the books that made up his library. There are some splendid XVIth-century volumes dealing with classical themes, as can be expected: an Italian version of Ovid's *Metamorphoses*, first editions of the works of Boscán and some of Garcilaso from 1543, *The Iliad* and Ficino's commentary to Plato's *Symposium*, plus *The City of the Sun* by Campanella. These books give tangible proof of Pantaleón's learning. I would add little more than a few contemporary authors and, needless to say, Corbalán's novels to a library of my own.

It took some doing, but I managed to convince Rodríguez Ventura to present *Relay* in Venusia. It'll probably be quite an occasion since it is Corbalán's birthplace. I'm afraid that they might not give us permission to do it.

So far so good, though. *Relay* is almost sold out despite less than flattering reviews. Sánchez Romero, one of the country's most prestigious critics, wrote in *La Nación* that there is a world of difference between *Relay* and *Senseless Days*, proof that the years in jail had a radical impact on the novelist. The Marcusi people don't seem to care very much, one way or the other, about the debate going on in the press. Who can blame them when the book is selling so well.

As I mentioned, I had dinner at the house of Isidoro Quiñonero, Don Pablo's friend. It was a real feast, but everything he told me about Corbalán was terribly upsetting, maybe the result of old personal rivalries. I have a hard time accepting that Corbalán was a small-minded opportunist, as Quiñonero portrays him. According to him, Corbalán used politics for his own personal agenda and never hesitated to manipulate even his closest friends to get what he wanted. His Pablo was not precisely a nice guy; quite the contrary, he seemed capable of virtually any depravity so long as he stood to benefit from it. I'm thoroughly baffled. I'd love to be able to talk with other people more impartial than Quiñonero, but here in Calipso it may not be possible since there is hardly anyone left from that time. They're either in jail or exiled abroad. Perhaps I'll be luckier in Venusia.

Quiñonero has adamantly urged me to stop inquiring into Corbalán's personal life. He claims that any such investigation could well attract the attention of the secret police and I might end up being thrown out of the country or, worse yet, in jail. Besides, it's very likely that I would be disillusioned by my findings. Quiñonero's daughter, and a friend of hers called Alberto Coma, thought otherwise and encouraged me to go on with my research. In their opinion Corbalán's overdose was not a suicide, as reported in the Italican press, but a murder which only the present military junta would have any interest in committing. It seems that Corbalán, with whom the government had made a pact of silence before setting him free—otherwise it's impossible to make sense of his reactionary statements—, was determined to speak out. So they killed him. That's what I believe, too. Quiñonero, however, remembers Pablo as an incurable neurotic who attempted suicide at least twice in the years when they were close.

Celia, time to go. I'll write again as soon as I get to Venusia and visit the house where he was born.

Warmest regards,

Teresa

P.S. This morning (the letter is from last night) I went to the Humanities Department at the University of Calipso. I wanted to check out Corbalán's records. They refused to show them to me since I didn't have written permission from the military authorities to view any documents. Such credentials are both required and, needless to say, not easily obtained.

Venusia, 19 December 1978

Dear Celia: I am well aware that in the creative process reality very often is merely a point of departure, perhaps even less than that. At times some inconsequential reference becomes the seed of a whole imaginary universe that seems real due to the internal coherence of artistic truth, which is also unlike that of life itself. But occasionally, when a work really moves us, we vehemently desire the story to be true; we want it to have taken place not just between the covers of a book but outside of them, on calendar pages; we want the characters to be people whom we might have met. And it is disturbing to realize the extent to which writers lie, how far they fake it. They are, indeed, capable of fabricating even the pain that they are really feeling, as Pessoa pointed out. Readers are frequently either naive or plainly stupid, which I've always considered closely related traits, never quite grasping the essential falseness of art.

I must confess that before leaving Barcelona I made a list of the names of all the streets, bars, buildings, factories, boarding houses, etc., that are mentioned in *Senseless Days* in the hope of identifying them as soon as I reached Calipso. I assumed that it made sense to seek out the parallels between life and literature within Latin American realism. Despite the Faustian motto that introduces the novel, «In the beginning there was action,» which has been given such subversive interpretations and serves as a warning to forget the particular names, I obstinately tried to locate every single one of them. It was an exercise in futility for which I, and not Corbalán, am to blame. Except for the main streets, all the other urban references are made up. Even the harbor area, magnificently and minutely described, does not exist. It never did. According to Alberto Coma, the professor of Italican literature that I met at Quiñonero's the other night, perhaps this was an attempt on Corbalán's part to avoid the possible reprisals that the novel might set off.

Yesterday I toured the outlying areas of Calipso: kilometer after kilometer of numbing poverty. During the ride Alberto told me about the horrible abuses suffered by political prisoners. Corbalán was no exception. He spent almost three years in the Calipso Military Stockade, one of the harshest in the state. Later he was transferred to the south, to the province of Nereidas, where thanks to international pressure his treatment improved. He was even allowed to write on one hundred page notebooks, in pencil, on the condition that he did not rip out a single page. Everything would be read and, needless to say, censored. Maybe that's why *Relay* is so different from *Senseless Days* and deals with a theme so far removed from the prison context in which it was written.

Alberto, who knows the city and its suburbs quite well, showed me the place where Corbalán seems to locate the shipyards (even though ships were never built in Calipso) which is where the events of October were planned. Curiously enough, at the time when Pablo was writing the novel that was the site of a rubber factory which was blown up shortly thereafter on government orders, under the pretext of urban redevelopment. For no overt reason other than this remote literary reference—its workers never actually revolted against Luzón—the factory became a symbol of resistance, some sort of mythical bastion. It was considered the breeding ground for an uprising that would break out the next time the military staged a coup. It was as if, in this way, the rebels were paying the debt that life owes to literature.

Here in Venusia I don't feel as threatened as in Calipso. I don't need to take so many precautions while checking out my long list of names and places. It's really Corbalán's life that I want to piece together, after all, not that of his characters. I'm feeling quite relieved that *Relay* takes place in an imaginary country, instead of in Itálica. That way I am not tempted to follow its spatial leads to try to determine the actual setting.

Venusia is a rather bland city. It does have, however, half a dozen splendid parks, much lusher than the ones in Calipso. When the hassle of the book presentation is over on Thursday, I'll devote all my remaining two weeks to what really brought me here.

Very fondly,

Teresa

Venusia, 23 December 1978

Dear Celia: Are my letters getting tiresome? If so, my apologies. I just realized that this is the third one this week. I hope they don't all arrive at once, that would be downright abusive! Writing to you is extremely therapeutic: it helps clarify things in my own mind and leaves me feeling rested. Actually, you are the only person that I've written to, aside from some cards to my parents and a few colleagues. Like any good introvert I'm not particularly given to easy intimacy, and my selection of friends is limited. However, this innate shyness has lately gone out the window by sheer force of circumstances. Celia, standing in for you has made me appreciate your talent. You are such a natural for these things, so thoroughly charming and intelligent. I envy you those qualities, that I have always wished for myself. I'm much too insecure, and my interest in literature may precisely stem from the fact that it is not life. Instead, it dwells in an ambiguous space that resembles life without having its destructive force that can be so terrifying.

Lately my whole life, not just my work, seems desperately literary as I try to find out everything there is to know about Corbalán. Not to worry, though. Despite my affinity to literary characters—often stronger than to flesh and blood specimens—I won't become one of them. I know myself and my limits very well, Celia, and do not intend to turn my life into an imitation of what happens in novels. Still, there are times when fiction offers very plausible explanations for life, for mine at least. Just four months ago I resorted to Bettina Brentano—do you know her? Goethe's romantic admirer— to better understand my mixed emotions after meeting Corbalán. But it's a long way from there to actually identifying with Bettina. She simply was in a similar situation: perfectly enthralled by a famous writer. Rereading her biography, recalling the obstacles she faced in order to meet him, shed a lot of light on my own relation with Pablo. But that's all.

These last few days have been pretty difficult, and not just because of all the work involved in preparing yet another book presentation. Here in Venusia, much more than in Calipso, there is overwhelming evidence of the terrible oppression which Itálica is suffering. Since I arrived, three days ago, I have the feeling that I'm being followed. I mentioned it to the Marcusi man, who very nicely offered to put me up in his house. For the time being I'm not going to accept. Maybe it's just my imagination. Whenever I analyze the situation objectively I tell myself that being a foreigner gives me a certain degree of immunity, that nothing can happen to me.

This morning I took pictures of the place where Pablo was born near downtown on Libertad Street—how's that for irony. It's a two story building that looks like it had a third one added not too long ago. I asked a woman who happened to be coming out if she knew Corbalán, and she said that twenty years ago the widow of someone by that name died there, on the first floor. Then the flat was sold. Since the woman was so nice, I asked if I could see her apartment, so now I have an idea of what Corbalán's looked like, assuming they were similar. I wanted to take pictures of the rooms but the look of sheer terror on the woman's face at the sight of the camera dissuaded me. I guess under the present circumstances her hospitality bordered on the heroic. Even though I look neither like a terrorist nor like an undercover agent, I'm still a stranger with too many questions for which there are precious few answers. I had to settle for rather vague, reticent replies. She had only seen Pablo a few times because when she moved into the building he no longer lived with his parents. Therefore, she had only a fleeting memory of him. She didn't like to read and so had never read his work. She had no idea where I could find his brothers. The woman was adamant about the fact that they were brothers and not sisters when I mentioned that I was under the impression that he was the only boy. As you can see, Celia, my findings are far from dazzling.

As soon as I can, I'll go out to the country estate that Corbalán's parents owned in Trebujar, about forty kilometers from Venusia.

That's all for now. I'll write soon.

Fondly,

Teresa

Venusia, 26 December 1978

Dear Celia: The regime appears on the verge of collapse. Last night at curfew there was a massive demonstration. The police charged blindly into the crowd killing three people and wounding hundreds of others. Today many stores are closed in mourning and solidarity. Even the rhetoric-filled official statements, that are being broadcast over the radio and on all three TV networks every half hour, describe the situation as critical. Naturally, under the circumstances there is no way to hold the book presentation ceremony for *Relay*. In the hotel lobby I overheard a man, who had just arrived from Calipso, mention that Sánchez Romero had been arrested. In short, things here are tense and most unpleasant. Only the knowledge that I wouldn't be able to return to Itálica any time soon keeps me from leaving immediately.

Yesterday after lunch I rented a car to drive to Trebujar. I figured that it would be easier to avoid being followed that way, and also more convenient altogether. Public transportation in Itálica is a real circus.

Trebujar is about fifty kilometers north of Venusia, as I think I already mentioned. The original property must have been huge but it's been parceled out. A very large colonial house is still standing, and there's a shade garden surrounded by high walls covered with wisteria, just as Corbalán described it. But Trebujar did not belong to his family but to a Venusian doctor called Gallego. His son, also a writer, met Pablo at the university. I asked to speak with him but the elderly lady who received me said that her brother had disappeared from Calipso eleven years ago. His name still figures in Amnesty International and Red Cross lists as a political prisoner but neither organization has been able to ascertain whether or not he is alive today.

Señora Gallego told me all sorts of stories. How the farm had been bought at the turn of the century by her grandfather, a Galician immigrant who had made a sizable fortune. How Trebujar had never belonged to Corbalán and, what's more, he had never even visited there. Antonio Gallego, who felt only contempt for him as a person and as a writer, would not have dreamed of inviting him. How, in fact, Gallego himself had written a book proving that *Senseless Days* had been plagiarized. As you can well imagine I was stunned. I asked Señora Gallego to lend me a copy and she promised to look for one, although she wasn't sure if there were any left among her brother's papers.

The little old lady was sweet and fragile, delicate as a porcelain figurine. She spoke in a sad but infinitely serene voice that touched me deeply. There was another woman there who stayed throughout my visit but never said a word, although she nodded in agreement. In spite of their mourning clothes these ladies were far from pathetic. They seemed to have assumed their pain, made it an essential part of themselves, like something borne since childhood. They offered me some *mate* tea in a large and sumptuously furnished room where we talked, as the edges of things blurred in the fading evening light.

I'm perfectly baffled, Celia. I cannot begin to fathom why Corbalán would give me false leads into his life, especially ones that could put me in personal jeopardy. Was he trying to pay for old sins? Or was it merely a monumental joke, some sort of trap for naive admirers? Maybe he just never imagined that I would make my way here to check out his memories. Or perhaps he simply wished to ridicule me before other scholars of his work, which would explain the switch in tapes. I need to look into one more thing: whether or not he worked for the Iberoamerican Publishing Company.

If the presentation of *Relay* is canceled and things continue to get worse here I'll return to Barcelona as soon as possible.

Love,

Teresa

Venusia, 29 December 1978

Dear Celia: My hunch was right, Corbalán was never employed by the Iberoamerican Publishing Company. I verified it for myself this morning since they keep rosters of contributors all the way back to the time when the firm was first established at the beginning of the century. Of course, it is possible that if he wrote only sporadically his name might not appear on many documents. There were a few old timers around and none of them remembered him. Nevertheless, if all he did was book reviews, his only contact might have been with the literary editor.

Faced with that dead end, and at a loss as to what else to do, I asked if Antonio Gallego had worked there. Lo and behold he had, between 1949 and 1955. A few people still remember him as polite, reserved, dependable and otherwise thoroughly nondescript.

I can't stop wondering why Corbalán kept referring to Antonio Gallego's life as his own. None of the explanations that I come up with persuade me. What role did Gallego play in his life, aside from letting him have some fun at my expense, that is. Perhaps my initial lie sparked a game of half truths. In a way his defense of lying might be a clue to keep in mind. Go back over my interview with him and you'll see it. But he certainly took it very far. Maybe he was really put off by my daring to compare myself to Bettina Brentano. Fine, so I wasn't really Bettina, but he was no Goethe himself either. You have no idea how awful I feel about all this. I have half a mind even to change the topic of my thesis, to destroy all I have done so far about *Relay*, to give way to my resentment and write that Corbalán was a fake and every bit as deserving of scorn as his acquaintances suggest. Quiñonero might be right when he claims that everything that Pablo touched he destroyed. On the other hand, things are either too grotesque or much too vulgar to ring true.

There must be a reason, a key to explain this whole mess. From now on I'll check out Antonio Gallego's life. Or try to. And, of course, I'll visit Trebujar again.

Late this morning Alberto Coma came by. It was a most pleasant and unexpected surprise. He warned me that the situation in Calipso is extremely critical and urged me to be careful, even with what I write to you. He advised me to stop digging around in both Corbalán's and Gallego's past, since both ended up in prison and, for that reason alone, any inquiries about them can be pretty dangerous. Alberto agrees that there's something fishy about Corbalán's attitude. He thinks that he didn't intend to ridicule me with his lies, but rather give me the means to unravel the mystery. Before I return to Barcelona I would like, at the very least, to have figured out the nature of the relationship between Corbalán and Gallego. Were they secret lovers as Alberto gleefully suggests?

Hugs,

Teresa

P.S. Celia, I just made one big discovery. Keep it a secret but don't forget it. Read only the capital letters of the following quote: Imagine A Moment New Over Time Consisting Of Remembrances Brave And Light And Numinous. This is what Corbalán wrote on my copy of *Senseless Days*. Do you realize the implications? Here's the next thread. I'll write soon.

12 January 1979

Dear Celia: I don't trust the mail at all, so I'm sending this via diplomatic channels of the Spanish Consulate in Venusia. Please, keep it in a safe place after you read it. Señora Gallego entrusted me with parts of it when I visited Trebujar. If anything happens to me, hand it over to the police and then try to have it published.

Celia, please, start proceedings to have the remains of the person who was buried in Cerdanyola as Corbalán exhumed. I have a plane ticket for Monday through New York and I can't wait to see you and explain so many things...

A warm embrace,

Teresa

PART III

I

They've been streaming out since before dawn, out of hiding places, lairs, burrows. They have left the sheds, the mucky rooms, the squalid huts. They have made their way from the slums, the outskirts, the urban beltway where the city runs out: where sewers empty, where putrid fumes hover, where excrement-filled waters stagnate.

They approach downtown from every direction, invading boulevards, fashionable avenues, shopping streets. In their wake doors close, metal shutters slam, bolts latch.

Suddenly, a roar. Unanimous. Deafening. One word, two syllables like blows, the second one more charged, like a closed fist to knock over, punch out, rip the enemy to shreds.

The roar is not a password or a political slogan. It's a name, unknown two years ago. Now, thanks to the clamor of so many voices, it becomes the only name. The name of salvation. The name of the deity, the hero, the caudillo, the keeper of the flame. Lu-zón, Lu-zón, Lu-zón.

From a distance it looks like a column of ants. *Marabunta*. Ant-men and women advancing like a disciplined army in attack formation. They have no eyes, no ears, no hands. Only noses. An animal sense to sniff out the tracks. Noses and mouths. Mouths. Throats. Vocal chords always, perpetually at work. A roar that bounces off walls, that climbs buildings, that leaps to roofs, that reaches up telephone poles and power lines. It rings in the air from the Plaza de la Independencia at the center of the city all the way back to the suburbs. Lu-zón, Lu-zón, Lu-zón. A roar that threatens to shatter the brittle tin planks of shanties, that rattles the peeling walls of cheap hovels.

Hundreds, thousands of voices chant that name, invoking his presence. Their faith and their consent consecrate him as the only guide, the only leader. They grant him all the powers. No one can silence them. Only he can when, heeding the call, he steps out onto the balcony of the Presidential Palace to answer the hoarse pleas of the mob, to profess his love with a voice that penetrates the prurient masses who, passive and submissive, offer him the possibility of the most obscene couplings, of the most sadistic abuses.

This is the daytime face of luzonism, a multiple face not without a certain beauty. Daytime face, blinding glitter. New order. Nationalism. Justice based on the fight against the oligarchy. That is the password, the golden-tipped arrow that pierces proletarian hearts with optimal results measured in decibels. Inflamed, deafening clapping that lasts long enough to let the leader put together his next phrase about commitment to the poor, the disenfranchised, the marginalized, the shirtless—clear link with the black and blue shirts that they are about to adopt. "Mussolini was a genius, but he made some grave mistakes that I will avoid," vows Luzón smiling, his arms reaching out as if to embrace the crowd, especially the old and the children. "They will be the only privileged class in Itálica, the only favored citizens."

Renewal. Recovery. Reaction. New force. New order. That is what Luzón offers in contrast to the coalition of *Unión Democrática*: an explosive mixture of communists, radicals, unionists, and conservatives, which aims to return to old ways, to obsolete laws, to the past instead of the future, a future that Itálica so desperately needs. "Reactionaries, passivists, traitors to history, enemies of their own country which goes forward, which must go forward over any and all hurdles."

They have been leaving the barracks since before dawn. Cautiously, protected by the milky morning light, they have been approaching. They take up positions, surround buildings. They advance under helmets and behind shields, with clubs in their hands and guns at their waists. They do not speak. They do not shout. They march onward with big, determined steps. Helmets shine in the sun, shields gleam. They cross the threshold. Screams are heard. Some people flee. They move on. They charge. They spread throughout the inner courtyard, the private offices. They enter the classrooms. They break chairs and benches. They enter the library, the seminar rooms. They tear up bookcases and throw books around as if they were bricks. They fight. They dodge. They shoot. They stop. They finally clear out. A cry, "Death to Luzón!," follows them to their dilapidated jeeps, spoils of European wars just recently unloaded at the harbor. They leave but don't quite go. They stay there surveying the scene. Thousands of eyes, like tentacles spread across the city to its very boundaries. Eyes like piercing rays of light that penetrate doors and windows, reaching into the most hidden nooks. Eyes that drill through walls to see everything, to control it all. Eyes that never close. Ears that listen always, forever present behind doors and park hedges, around corners. Any rustle can be subversive. Any word can signal a code. The slightest hint is sufficient to unmask an enemy.

Sewer-like burble, fetid stench of backwaters, of rotting carcasses, of innards and guts... an underground labyrinth, tunnels and recesses, chambers that shudder with each subway train, the surging of foul waters rushing into the sea, the scurrying of rats. I see the slimy trace of a slug down the flaking wall. A slug that has left its imprint on my forehead, next to my mouth, on my face which is the face of revulsion. My back is sliced by whiplashings. Rabid dogs bite me still. My buttocks burn on from the heat of cigarettes.

They took him one morning during a routine check of the university. They accused him of subversion, of being an anti-Luzón agitator on Moscow's payroll. They don't like his articles. Besides, he writes for an opposition newspaper. Even though he's never signed them, either with his name or with a pseudonym, it's not difficult to figure out who is crouching between the poisoned lines. He blatantly attacks the government under any pretext, when writing about daily life, about aspects of foreign policy, about anything not yet under the scrutiny of the censors. Still, it is remarkable that this subversive column, where Marxist ideas are propounded, should appear in a conservative publication. *El Día* is owned by the Paz family. His long-standing friendship with them is based on their common hatred for the dictator and the adherence to some basic principles, often unrelated except for the fundamental aim of opposing Luzón. But there is more. Much more. Other bonds, so secret that only he knows of them: the color of a pair of eyes, the voluptuousness of a kiss, the solemn well-shaped thighs under sheer silk. Autumn was at its peak that first time: a splendid body in his arms and the impression of having come from very far away. As if every one of his steps throughout his entire life could be counted in kilometers, justified only because they led him here, to this moment, to these feelings. As if beyond all the political acts or literary successes, life had meaning only for having allowed him that unique instant. He seemed to acquire another sense that reached beyond touch, sight, hearing, smell, and taste. A new and more intense one, a synthesis of all the others with which to perceive the plenitude of that hour, its distinctness, that only forgotten words, tainted words from a vocabulary already rejected, words like beatitude or grace, could help define.

Blanca Alvarado de Paz. Yes, Señora de Paz herself, who holds out her hand with a slight tilt to make it easier to kiss. A pale, refined hand, impeccably manicured and sprinkled with rings. Her hand, light as a wing brushing his brow, his eyelids, and coming to rest captive of his sex.

Blanca, Blanca. A name like an amulet blanched by kisses; a colorless name that encompasses all colors. He whispers it softly, thinks it to himself, carves it with his nails into the damp, peeling walls. A name to hold tightly in his hands against his chest like a jewel, to hang around his neck like a locket, or wave like a flag.

They had been lovers for barely four months even though they had known each other for about two years, since Señor Paz was kind enough to invite him for tea to show him his private library. Blanca joined only briefly, just for the greetings, and left again under some trite excuse. It was later, when Paz offered him the post of librarian, that he got to know her. And one fine day—or one awful day, he always corrected himself—he realized that he would give his life, everything he was and everything he had, all he could ever hope to be, fame, fortune, glory, prestige, power, anything in exchange for her love. It was a short siege. He was constantly tormented by guilt about betraying a friend, by having to hide his feelings, by the cordial aloofness with which she treated him before family and servants. They had precious few chances to meet alone. Occasionally he took her to a bar on the outskirts, where they held hands and listened to tangos whose lyrics seemed vaguely to refer to them. Other times they walked around the port, down to the loading docks. He would tell her pirate stories that he had heard from his grandfather, a Galician captain who landed in Calipso at the beginning of the century. Blanca listened without blinking, and both avoided any references to ships or ocean liners because neither wanted to be the first to bring up the possibility of running away together, and they skirted even the mere mention of objects that would serve that purpose. How could he, penniless student, aspiring writer, unknown journalist, powerless, without connections in Europe or acquaintances in Madrid, Paris, or London, push Blanca to undertake such an adventure? But the fact that she belonged to another man was unbearable. He respected Paz, who had done him nothing but good; yet this made it even worse. He would have liked it so much better if Paz had been a jerk, a real bastard who abused Blanca. But no such luck. Quite the opposite. Overwhelmed by remorse he would imagine an alternative scenario: Paz was nothing but a capitalist who opposed Luzón only to defend his own interests. He wished he didn't know him, that he had met Blanca through someone else. But he was not about to give her up whatever the circumstances. His love took precedence over everything, even over guilt, that hateful word. The guilt that flooded him whenever he unlocked a hotel room disappeared as soon as they began their love games in strange beds that Blanca felt rather squeamish about, not so much because of the mortal sin she was committing but because of the diseases that could be picked up from those not excessively clean sheets. But Blanca was aware that she was participating in a strange ritual of simultaneous joy and pain: a deed that demanded confession, a communion that brought her to a state of total grace. Her love for that idealistic young dreamer took her back thirty years to her childhood innocence, to moments of timeless beauty and perfection that she feared forever gone in her maturity. She recoiled before the sordidness of the rooms, but this was understandable in someone who had attended Swiss boarding schools and had always slept and loved on immaculately white linens, embroidered with initials and sometimes even crowns. She still kept some from the XVIIIth century that had belonged to her Spanish great-grandmother who joined her Castilian title of nobility to the landed wealth of her *criollo* husband. Unfortunately, all titles had been abolished at the end of the colonial period by the constitution that established Itálica as an independent nation. It was only natural, then, for her to cringe at soiled linens. But her love was above any physical or moral scruple and Blanca Alvarado de Paz, like a vestal on the sacrificial altar, gave herself devoutly, forgetting even the roughness of the sheets, frayed from so much use.

Blanca was the light. She dispersed the shadows in his cell, chased away the ghosts, gave back to the walls their true contours, the speckled, cracked texture that no longer seemed like menacing mouths, packs of preying nightbirds, mountain ranges crashing down on his cot.

Blanca's body naked next to his. Under it. The spasms of lovemaking. The pulsating blood, rushing through their veins as their hearts pounded in unison. His mouth over Blanca's, breathing each other's breaths, drinking her thirst, moistening with her saliva his dried out gums and the tongue that sought hers to do battle anew, to conquer that cove guarded by glistening stones, signposts of her smile, wet with foam from diminutive waves. Calm sea, dark and gleamless, through which only two pink and pliant ships move, advance and retreat as they are assailed; they twist and turn following their captain's orders or let themselves drift with the current, fearless of obstacles, ignoring the warnings of beached or sunken galleons.

The memory of that battle always helped him wage the other one, harsher but less perilous: whiplashes, pointed tips that gore the flesh of his ribcage exposing the bones. Razor sharp scalpels. Needles piercing his nipples.

Crushing blows from boxing champions trained in clandestine rings, in the dark tunneled barracks of the *luzonista* armed forces. Countless elbows, knees, boot-clad feet stomping and kicking stomachs, chests, genitals. I gasp for air but my mouth is far too small. I can't do it. Gritty blood clots fill my throat, my lips are cracked, my gums are bleeding. I can't breathe, I'm choking. Blanca's memory, Blanca's kisses. I can't get enough air. I can't get my breath. I can't.

II

He walked briskly, instinctively, along the streets without paying much attention to anything or anyone, until he reached Briseida Park. He found a bench and sat down. He fixed his eyes on the multicolored light filtering through the tree branches and splashing onto the ground. It looked as if someone sitting by a tiny, invisible window up high was passing the time aiming various light bulbs on that particular place, the way he had seen it done at the theater when he was a child. He rubbed his eyelids with a mechanical gesture. His eyes had grown used to the darkness of the cell and were now easily bothered by light. He felt glad for the golden shades of autumn, for the soft pastels that caressed his retina. He would not have been able to stand the blinding glare of a summer day outlining each tree, every branch. He looked around. The season was way ahead of the calendar. Yellowish leaves whirled in the streets groaning like arthritic old ladies whenever they were scattered by a gust of wind. In the sky, flocks of birds drew easily decipherable hieroglyphs: we're off to warmer climates.

During those first few moments of freedom, while crossing the street at its narrowest point to quickly distance himself from the prison, he felt a strong urge to speak, to start chatting with the first person who would listen and not take each one of his words as a provocation, a denunciation, a sign of criminal subversive activity. The fear of finding in that randomly-chosen face—an innocent one undoubtedly—the features of his tormentors, made him abandon the idea. He was apprehensive about discovering their likeness even in those faces he loved best.

Sitting at the park he decided to make every effort to put those months behind, even though he knew for a fact that his scars would never completely heal. He gave himself an hour, one more hour to settle all his doubts. He considered looking up his fellow conspirators, assuming they still met at the same place, but dismissed the idea because it seemed too risky. Maybe they had released him so suddenly, so unexpectedly, in order to follow him, to use him as bait. He could also not go see Blanca looking like that, it would be self-defeating. Taking the train to Venusia and holing up at his parents' presented all sorts of difficulties as well, and it would entail postponing his reunion with Blanca. He resolved to stay in Calipso. He figured that the landlady probably still kept his trunk and his suitcases in spite of his vanishing act. After all, he had never owed her any money. Just the opposite, he had always paid on time and on several occasions had even helped her through a tight spot by paying in advance. He pondered the possibility of asking her for shelter for a few days while he contemplated his next move: stay in Calipso or leave the city for a period of time. He needed to rest free from the worry that at any moment they might arrest him once more. He could not bear the thought of going back to prison so soon. He needed a truce, a vacation, a leave. Maybe they would consider him a coward. And maybe he was. But he had no strength left to hold up under questioning, no shred of skin unmarked by lashings and torture. More than anything, he yearned to see Blanca, to stay with Blanca for a long time. He missed her now more than ever, more than when he was in jail, more desperately even, for the same reason that someone coming back to life needs nourishment more than someone who is dying.

He left the park. The last thing he wanted to do was take the subway so he headed towards Barrientos Road. He chose the busiest streets in order to get lost in the crowds. He was afraid that his famished, gaunt look would give him away. No one likes an ex-con, even when it happens to be a political prisoner. He caught a glimpse of a familiar face: Campuzano. He started to approach him, but backed away when he realized that the other did not react to him. They had worked together organizing Marxist cells at the university. They were comrades if not friends. Perhaps Campuzano was preoccupied; or perhaps he decided not to acknowledge him for reasons of personal safety; or, simply, he had not recognized him. I've lost weight and grown a beard. That must be it, the beard! They would not let me shave. He must shave at once. All Italican men shaved. Beards were a giveaway. As he turned the corner of Yrigoyen Street he came face to face with the mirror of a confectioner's shop, one of those huge mirrors that ladies check before going in for their afternoon tea, to make sure that every hair is in place. He could not resist the temptation. What he saw alarmed him: his eyes were sunken, ringed with purplish circles, greasy strands of hair fell inside the collar of the jacket that, like his pants, just hung on him. He knew Blanca would be horrified if she saw him like that. He almost ran to the boarding house and had to stop to catch his breath under a balcony that had a sign on it: «Rooms.» Then he climbed the stairs. The door was open.

Señora Acosta kissed him profusely. He had always hated kisses until he felt Blanca's lips. Since then he doubly hated those that did not come from her. So the slimy mass of the landlady's mouth brought to mind the slugs that slid about his cell and he shuddered.

"How good to see you. My God, this is wonderful. It was about time. Thank heaven you're out. But why did they get you? Of all people, you who wouldn't hurt a fly.... Politics, politics... But Luzón means well, really.... This is great!"

She took his face into her hands and kissed him some more with loud slurping noises. He was helpless to stop that attack of affection. He came close to fleeing the same way he had come. He found her wordiness and her physical expression of delight offensive.

"We have missed you around here. You can believe that. I wanted to hold the room for you but, you know, times are hard and my husband made me rent it. What if he doesn't come back when they let him out? he said to me. What if he decides to find another place? Do you know that *El Día* shut down? It's supposedly because of lack of paper... I saved the last few issues for you. Your column was still being published under the same title, but someone was signing it... I can't remember his name. Wait just a second and I'll get them. They're right here."

Soledad Acosta crammed her overflowing frame into a closet built under the stairwell that led to the second floor, where she and her husband had their quarters.

"Here you go. They're all for you. I don't need them. I have enough others to wrap things in and they're not very good for kindling because they give off too much smoke; in any case, I use only two sheets at a time in the kitchen. Keep them and notice the difference. I'm no expert, but your articles were better. More refined, more elevated... My husband said so himself."

The stack was heavy. He dropped it on a chair and picked one out at random. He was eager to know who had signed his column, to find out who had taken his place. Briefly he thought it might be Blanca but immediately realized that notion was too farfetched. Señora de Paz never took part either in public life or in her husband's business. She was not about to raise eyebrows by doing so in this precise instance, on his behalf. Yes, the title was the same, although the column was shorter and it had been moved to a different page. It was signed by Pablo Corbalán. He became livid. Why did it have to be Corbalán? He didn't like that guy, so arrogant and presumptuous, so contentious, always trying to get one-up on others, forever giving orders and meddling in other people's lives as if he knew better... But how did that come about, if he had no contact with the newspaper, if he didn't even know Paz? Corbalán was a writer all right, but he never did any journalism which he considered sloppy work, for nitwits only. Actually, Gallego had to admit it, the column was quite powerful and eloquent, not half bad at all. Señora Acosta interrupted him.

"Did you find it? What's the name of the person who signed it? Conalán? Cornalán?"

"Corbalán. Pablo Corbalán."

"That's it. That's why it was so familiar. It's the man who took your trunk and your suitcases... I haven't told you about that yet... He came around ten days after you disappeared and inquired if you owed anything..."

"Are you positive it was Corbalán?"

"Almost sure. Anyway, he gave me a card with his name and address... It's upstairs. I put it on the night table... And I can tell you what he looked like: tall, more or less like you, the same color hair... His nose was a little longer than yours... A very nice looking man, if I may say so. There was a certain resemblance. Are the two of you related?"

"Not remotely. I would very much like to take a shower... but this is all I have..."

He pulled some coins out of his pocket, mostly small change.

"I can't even leave my luggage as security since, according to you, it's not here."

"For heaven's sake, Antonio," she clucked like a broody hen, "for heaven's sake. We've known each other for a long time. There's no problem. I'll run the bath myself. If you'd like a clean change of clothes you can have my brother-in-law's suit, may he rest in peace. It's about the right size. It's so good to see you that it had completely slipped my mind... We were just distraught. He died last month, after falling off a crane. And, to tell you the truth, I hated to have him buried with his new suit. He'd had it made just last winter, he only got to wear it once..."

There was no answer when he dialed the number on Corbalán's card. He had no alternative but to accept Soledad Acosta's offer and put on the dark suit that made him look like a dressed-up hick on his way to a funeral. He headed out towards the Champs Elysées.

Perhaps it would have been better to call first before showing up out of the blue, but he had waited five whole months and now just could not wait any longer. Besides, if he called they would likely invite him to tea and, grateful as he might be for such a treat, he did not want to postpone the meeting until four or five in the afternoon.

It was ten o'clock. Señor Paz had probably left already for the office. Aside from *El Día* he also controlled *La Prensa*, another opposition newspaper that was still being published in spite of certain difficulties. He bought a copy at a corner stand. Paz was a meticulous man of predictable habits who enjoyed being directly in charge of his business affairs.

Blanca must still be in her bedroom, wearing the blue silk kimono embroidered in gold that her husband had brought her from Japan.

"I'd give anything to be able to see you when you're alone."

"But if you were with me I'd no longer be alone, we'd be together, I'd be with you..."

"What I want is to see you without you being aware of me, without you being able to see me."

"Ahhhh, you want to peep!"

"No, that's not it. I'd like to see you without being conscious that I am seeing you, as if you and I were one and the same person with the ability to stand apart, to see you without stepping outside myself."

"The things you say, darling..."

It was usually after making love that he would ask her to tell him about what she did on any given day, from morning until night, without omitting the most insignificant details. He wanted to share in her life even if vicariously. This way he could imagine her every minute, follow her through her varied activities with little margin for error. Perhaps today he might have the privilege of seeing her in that silk robe, of touching the sensuous material, of relishing her face without make-up and her chestnut hair loose on her shoulders. She might, after such a long separation, rush down to see him without wasting any time getting dressed. After all he was a friend of the family, he had been in prison, he had endured terrible tortures and not given out a shred of information. What could be more natural than having the lady of the house see him without a moment's hesitation?

He smiled to himself imagining the scene. He walked faster. He was happy. He felt very much the hero, in a way. «And the most beautiful woman smiled at the bravest of the victors.» Blanca was gorgeous, the fairest of them all, but he belonged to the vanquished, the losers, dressed as he was in the clothes of a dead bricklayer... But maybe being the loser was, in this instance, an advantage; it put him in a different category, granted him a certain aura that none of the *luzonistas* who eyed Blanca lustfully at parties or plays possessed. No, he would not trade places with any of the victors. Not even with Luzón himself. Nor with Paz. Blanca loved him.

They assured him that Señora de Paz was not home. She had gone out. They did not know when she would re-

turn. He better not wait around. Señor Paz, as was his cus-
tom, had gone to *La Prensa*.

The maid treated him with a certain diffidence. She
did not even ask him to come in. She must not be aware
that I've been in prison. Makes sense. Why should she
know? It would have been foolish to mention it in front
of her. She might be a *luzonista*.

He made up his mind to wait for Blanca on the street.
He moved away from the house so as not to arouse suspi-
cion and went in search of a spot from where to watch
without being seen by the servants. At the end of the block
there was a small tree-lined park with slides and swings,
put there on explicit orders from Señora de Luzón for the
sake of destitute children. It had been built in this particular section of town by mistake. Rich kids had no use for
such installations. They had their own yards, their own
swing sets, so the park sat mostly empty. Only a round-
faced little girl, with pock marks and skinny legs that stuck
out from under a frayed skirt, was at the playground.
When she saw him coming she jumped off and scurried
away. He tried to stop her, saying entreatingly "Don't go.
Do you want to play with me?" but the child had already
turned the corner and was out of sight. He felt a wave of
regret. He would have liked to chat with her. It had been
so long since he had had any contact with a child. Perhaps
her mother had warned her not to speak to strangers. It
wouldn't surprise me, given the times. In a way, I'm the
one who should leave since I'm the one who trespassed
into her territory. But he stayed put. He found a bench. Sat
down. Opened the newspaper. Stared at the headlines. He
began to read them but changed his mind. If he got involved with the news he would not notice Blanca's
arrival. Besides, he could not follow, he was too excited to
be able to concentrate. Perhaps she would come back soon.
Where could she have gone? To the dress-maker, the

hairdresser, shopping? This feminine world was completely foreign to him and he used to find it shallow until he fell in love with Blanca. Still, it was hard for him to fathom how she could bear to spend, not to say enjoy, whole mornings with her head covered with curlers, or having clothes fitted while partaking of the gossip usual in those establishments. The few times he had brought up the topic she had silenced him with kisses and had smilingly assured him that men, including him who was so different from all the others, were incapable of appreciating the fact that women needed a private space in which to pay homage to the body and to the demands for beauty that men themselves had imposed.

"Would you still love me if you found me ugly?"

"I love you the way you are. You could never be otherwise."

But he was jealous of the time she spent on her hair, her clothes. He wished for her a life less cluttered, less dependent on the opinion of others. He would like it better if she was somewhat less spectacular, less the main focus of attention. It incensed him no end to know that others desired her. Besides, Blanca's hectic social schedule kept them apart. He would never be able to offer her a life of such prominence if she were ever to leave with him. At some point he had become obsessed with this idea and often promised himself that he would ask her to abandon everything the moment he saw her. But each time he put it off. Where to escape? With what means? He decided to think about something else. He was determined to block out all depressing thoughts. Any time now he would see her. He would hold her in his arms again. He went over all the other errands he had to run that day. First he had to find Corbalán and get his things back. Why on earth did he ever take them, in the first place? And he would probably even have to thank him for going to so much trouble, for his concern. Corbalán must have figured that the police would search his place, go through his stuff, and so he took it into safekeeping. He was particularly intent on recovering his books, the novel he had been working on, the notes for future projects, the poems dedicated to Blanca. Now that so much time had elapsed he would read it all with increased objectivity, with the necessary distance to find the faults and correct them. He had written about one hundred pages of the novel and felt determined to finish it. He would work on it consistently through the winter in order to have it done before summer. Then he would look for a publisher. It would naturally be dedicated to Blanca, even if her name did not appear or was hidden under some nickname.

He planned to go back to school and finish his degree. He needed to take only two more courses. His parents would be delighted. He was looking forward to seeing them. He had not been to Venusia in over a year. Since the last elections. It had been memorable. His father was leading a demonstration at the Sarmiento Theater while he and his comrades rallied at the Itálica Theater. They had agreed not to attack each other when they both decided to run for public office. That night at dinner Doctor Romualdo Gallego confessed to his son that he had never, in his entire life, been more distraught than the day he found out that the young man had become a member of the Communist Party.

The image of his father's contorted features emerges amid the whirling memories and brings a smile to his face.

"Would you rather have me be a *luzonista*?"

"No, not that. Never."

The answer was unequivocal. At the same time the old man stared at him over his glasses, scrutinizing him fixedly but without a trace of animosity, as if trying to diagnose a lump on the skin of one of his patients. Then, abruptly changing topics and relaxing his face as he picked up a cup of consommé, the father began extolling the virtues of a good Galician stew and wondering why the canneries of Vigo had never thought of packaging it for export to Itálica and Argentina.

"Get your radical friends to include that proposal in the platform. If you win the election you can send the Galicians some wheat in exchange... Mention this to any Galician immigrant and he'll be sure to vote for you."

My thoughts turn to food. I'm hungry. I'll suggest to Blanca to eat at a restaurant in the outskirts... I guess that won't do, since I don't have a penny. And besides, she has never agreed to eat with me.

"I didn't know you had a girlfriend."

"What makes you say that, mamá?"

"I saw a photograph on your desk..."

"Well, yes. I'm in love."

"What's her name? When do we meet her?"

"Her name is Blanca."

"And how old is she?"

"A few years older than me."

"Oh, I don't like that at all. Just how many is that?"

"Not that many..."

"I presume you know the exact figure...?"

"Yes, mamá, twelve."

Now it's his mother's turn to be aghast. She studies him wordlessly, her face cupped by long-fingered hands similar to Blanca's. They are sitting at the far end of the garden in Trebujar, next to an old myrrh tree, by the wall which in November gets covered with wisteria blossoms. Señora Gallego shakes her head, in a familiar gesture that conveys surprise or distress.

He should call them long distance this very day to let them know he is out, to tell them that he will visit soon, and to have them wire him some money urgently. He can't even buy a train ticket right now... And while he waits for the check to bail him out he will go and see his German students. It is quite likely that they no longer need his services. They have probably found another teacher already. But they still owe him a month's fees. He was arrested on the 28th. He will stop by the academy this afternoon. Unfortunately the newspaper doesn't owe him much, barely for seven or eight articles. Anyway, he is not going to demand the money, it would be tacky to do so now that they have been shut down. Paz has always been generous with him. Thanks to him he met Blanca. He should visit him later this morning. He will say that he stopped by the house first to say hello to his wife. Just good manners. He hates the constant need to pretend. Ever since he took up with Blanca he has been avoiding Paz. He feels this is the least cynical stance. But today there is no choice. He must stop by the offices of *La Prensa*. He has to express his condolences for the demise of *El Día* and, aside from that, he wants to know why Corbalán took his place. Paz is likely to ask him to write something for *La Prensa* and that would be good for him, even though he just might decline the offer. Things would be so much easier if he could confess the truth: that he is desperately in love—just like Paz himself must have been twenty years ago—with his wife.

Using the tip of one of his shoes, the only things he is wearing that actually belong to him, he writes Blanca's name on the sandy ground of the park. It is a habit he has had since he was a kid when he would scribble all over: the floor, the walls, anything. He would scratch with the edge of a pocket knife until the surface splintered. His mother always scolded him for this behavior. Just like a little street urchin, she would say.

Blanca. A name written at his feet. He draws a circle around it. Please hurry, Blanca. I'm here, they've finally let me go. I'm here and I'm waiting for you. It's been five months, five long, five unending months without you, Blanca. I didn't stop thinking about you one single day. I want you. I know you love me, I know you have waited too, but I need to hear you say it, I need for you to tell me. What if Blanca has forgotten me? What if she's decided to leave me? I haven't heard a word from her all these months. No letters, no messages. Nothing. But no. No. Blanca was in love with him. And he believed in Blanca. He had faith in her love even though at the beginning it had seemed much too wonderful to be true, altogether like one of those miracles that one reads about in saints' biographies. Why him? What merits did he have, what qualities did he possess, what extraordinary virtues made him worthy of Blanca's love?

Suddenly he leapt up. He had seen her at the opposite end of the street speaking animatedly with an older lady that he did not recognize. He waved at her but she must not have seen him since there was no response. He waited a few seconds after she had gone through the gate and then he rushed to the house and rang the bell. He was afraid of choking on his own voice out of sheer emotion.

"Señora de Paz, please."

"I already told you she wasn't home."

"That's not so. I just saw her arrive. Please let her know I'm here."

The maid had a slightly mocking air that disturbed him. She did not ask him in. She left him standing in the foyer and was even so rude as to leave the front door open.

Blanca came at once. She was still wearing a coat and carrying her purse. She was pale. She gave him her hand and he kissed it repeatedly.

"How are you? I'm glad to see you. When did you get out?"

He stared at her, still unable to believe that she was there before him. He had to force his eyes wide open and concentrate on the paintings by Fongtehbern, on the empire chairs, on the valuable console centered against a back wall, to absorb the fact that he was no longer in his cell, that he really had made his way out, right into this dream. He wanted to embrace her, to rest his head softly on her lap and make up for the thirty six hundred hours he had spent without seeing her, without touching her, without hearing from her. He needed to sink into her mouth and recover the taste of her tongue, the scent of her body. He wanted to make love to her to the point of exhaustion.

"I was yearning to see you..."

She showed him into the colonial-style room where she liked to see her close friends. It was there, he remembered distinctly, that she had agreed to their first meeting.

"It's been awful. You can't begin to imagine it. And I was dying to see you. I know there was nothing you could do to help me..."

There was silence. Blanca was sitting across from him fidgeting with her bracelets. Then she stood up and took off her coat.

"It's kind of warm for this time of year, don't you think?... Odd autumn we're having."

"Do you still love me? Please tell me, I need to hear it. Did you think about me?"

"Shhh, not so loud, please, someone could hear you."

This was definitely not the welcome that he had in mind.

"Blanca, what's the matter? What is it, don't you love me anymore?"

Blanca continued playing around with her bracelets, which made a tinny sound. Her eyes remained glued to her left wrist. Without looking up, and in a very small voice she declared the encounter over.

"I'd like you to go now... I know this is an awkward moment to say this, but we cannot go on. It's better to tell you clearly so that you will not insist."

He gaped at her in utter astonishment. If this was a joke, it was in very bad taste. Or was it a whim? Some kind of test that he had to pass to prove himself? There had been a few of those before. Except this time it was unwarranted. And he was not about to play along. He stood up and went to her. He tried to touch her hands. She pulled away.

"I can't believe you. Would you care to explain."

"We can't go on. We simply cannot."

The words shot out of her mouth. Nothing could have been as shattering. The lashings, the prod, the shocks, nothing had ever hurt so badly.

"Did your husband find out? Did someone tell him?"

"Please, go. I don't want to cause you any more pain. Go, please."

III

Five years later an item in the *Diario de Venusia* violently jerked him back to the time after his release from prison, to the dark and empty days after he lost Blanca. He had wasted those five years trying to come up with a reason, analyzing their relationship with stubborn thoroughness in search of a clue, any hint that might explain why she had left him. If constantly forcing memory on one single issue, around one concrete and hopeless episode, could cause it to atrophy, he would have achieved a state of total amnesia. But now, thanks to what he had just read, he felt sure he could finally pull out the needles of uncertainty that had tortured him for so long. Swearing to himself that this would be the last time, he concentrated during the following week with the intensity of someone watching through the microscope the culture of a bacteria that would save the human race from a devastating epidemic. And, even though he needed no props for this endeavor, he pulled out of a desk drawer the concrete proofs of his failure: a large bluish envelope containing other smaller ones addressed in shaky handwriting to Señora Blanca Alvarado de Paz, which were returned to him, unopened, as promptly as they had been delivered. He emptied the contents of yet another faded folder that had once been bright red. He examined them all: poems that had kept him up entire nights, drafts of letters never sent, scribbled notes outlining his final wishes, dried flowers, bougainvilleas and roses from Blanca's garden picked on the street while waiting for her in vain. Then he carefully unfolded a map of Calipso and tacked it to the wall. There were red circles drawn around three different areas: one to the north of the city, one downtown, and one near the harbor. These were the settings for his own private tragedy. The streets that led from his boarding house to the Paz residence, to Corbalán's house, and to the port area had been outlined in black. The purple markings followed Blanca's preferred routes, the ones way outside of town that she chose for their walks precisely because it was unlikely that any of her many friends would be there. He had starred the places discovered together, as if they offered spectacular views, artistic or historical treasures not to be missed by a single tourist. More than once he had playfully joked with Blanca that these places would one day figure in Calipso tourist guides despite their relative lack of natural beauty and the total absence of historical significance. They would be included simply because in them she had loved the writer that would make her immortal.

They first made love in a room rented by the hour in some sleazy dive. It had no windows, the furniture was hideous, the large mirrors reflected mostly their own dirt. Nevertheless, on the landscape of their relationship, it took on the qualities of a Gothic cathedral. The open fields where they strolled, barren grounds suited only for this-tles and nettles, became exuberant gardens or splendid parks. The seedy harbor cafes, dank and dilapidated, reeking thickly and populated by whores past their prime, stood out like national monuments. But the highest ranking was reserved for the place where they had gone that first afternoon that she agreed to go out with him: a noisy tavern with a raspy-voiced tango singer on the north basin, where one could watch the docking maneuvers of merchant ships. It was there also that on subsequent afternoons Blanca gradually revealed to him in her warmest and most intimate tone the feelings he evoked in her: the mixture of uneasiness and calm, the longing and the boundless desire—her very words—and the dreaminess, the impulse to sleep with abandon in his arms. It was there that she finally admitted—with much hesitation, circumlocution and embarrassment—that she loved him too. But the five star ranking was later removed since that tavern was also the site of their last meeting. A meeting she was forced to accept to prevent him from calling constantly, from pleading with her over and over sometimes even to the point of threatening. A meeting she attended looking wan and weary. It was a Blanca different from the one he had known, a tense and awkward woman who sat briefly by his side and glanced at him with an indifference more offensive than contempt or resentment, a glance devoid of any hint of her former tenderness. His feverish words, laden with longing and supplication, the memories of so many joyful hours together, the promise of future happiness, all failed to persuade her to either postpone her decision or sweeten the parting.

"There's no use. Please don't insist. I don't want to see you again."

"But why? What happened?"

"I don't love you anymore."

That simple: she didn't love him anymore. Finally it was clear. The infatuation had just blown over. Nothing tied her to him. Yet she had loved him intensely, even in spite of herself, and had been utterly desolate when he was jailed, thinking she might never see him again. She went so far as to risk asking her husband to intercede in his favor. He knew influential people who might try to have him released. But then things happened—she repeated absently—things that convinced her of her folly. And when he demanded to know what things she meant, she said only that she had promised herself not to talk to him about them. Perhaps in a few years, if they happened to run into each other, perhaps then the time would be right. If she were to tell him now she was positive he would hate her. When he swore that he would never question her again and asked that they remain friends, that they get together occasionally, that she give him a chance to win her back slowly, to make her fall in love with him once more, she got up to leave. When he took her arm and attempted to make her sit back down, she pushed him away violently. She did not kiss him good-bye, did not shake his hand. She did, however, forcefully demand that he stay put and finish his drink; she ordered him not to follow her or he would regret it for the rest of his life.

He watched her rush out into the fine drizzle that was soaking the city, her coat collar turned up, her hair under a silk scarf. From behind the steamed-up windows he saw her fade in the distance, amid the wailing of sirens, the rattling of cargo ships, the yapping of seagulls, the crashing of waves against the breakers. For a few seconds he was able to follow her frail figure into a gray horizon surrounded by hangars and cranes until she finally disappeared behind the harbor's huge silos. He gulped down the last of the gin, debating whether to comply with her request and stay a while or follow her at a distance and protect her from all the dangers lurking out there. Blanca chased down by sailors; Blanca humiliated, robbed, raped, murdered on the docks, leaving a puddle of blood where anemones would bloom.

His recollection of these events inevitably led back to Señora Acosta who, in his most deranged fantasies, had played the part of grotesque matron of honor to Blanca. Still today he regretted having taken her into his confidence, which he did only out of the need to reach Blanca, to communicate with her at any cost. Over the phone the landlady's voice raised fewer suspicions than his own. But this trick did not work either. Only once did Blanca come to the phone for a short and unpleasant exchange and she finally just hung up on him. The complicity with her guest, who for the moment was a freeloader, had evoked in Señora Acosta a surge of nostalgia for her wild single days. She recalled a certain man who walked like Gallego, and who had possessed her twenty times in one night all the while grunting like a panther. Thinking that perhaps fate was giving her another chance at love, Soledad Acosta decided to take the initiative and slip into her guest's room clad in her sexiest nightie. Antonio Gallego had nearly had enough of Señora Acosta's frequent innuendoes, which seemed to parody his feelings for Blanca. Every time the landlady tried to comfort him by pressing his head against the quivering mass of flesh that spilled out of her low-cut dresses, he came near to puking. She remained oblivious to his reaction. Soledad Acosta liked to question Gallego about his relation with Blanca, and became clearly aroused probing their degree of intimacy. Gallego answered evasively since the last thing in the world he wanted was to open his heart to that cow of a woman. The night that the landlady, taking advantage of her husband's absence, decided to go for broke and waited in Antonio's bed, he figured it was time to make a final exit. But before doing so he allowed himself the experience of pure nausea, just like with the slugs in his prison cell, as he felt a slimy caress over his body and on his genitals that tried, gently at first and then with undisguised fury, to overcome his rejection.

"I'm not surprised that she left you," scoffed Soledad Acosta later that night, attempting to humiliate him, as she covered her overflowing flab with an enormous robe apt for a truck driver in drag. Antonio Gallego splattered bile and the remains of his dinner on the bedspread before slamming the door. He swore never to set foot in that house again and cursed the landlady for making him wish for a hatchet, or a freshly sharpened kitchen knife, to chop her into pieces and treat stray dogs and vultures to a feast.

In spite of the still bitter taste, of the disgust distilled from images of an almost exemplary ugliness, now five years later he thinks for the first time that perhaps he was unfair to the poor fat slob whose main fault was to have loved him, to have dared desire him. This was the key point. If the landlady had never offered herself maybe he would have continued to accept her affection, even though he was aware that he could never return it. But the fact that she took the initiative—egged on, he was positive, by the new law granting women the right to vote and run for office—continued to seem to him thoroughly unacceptable. He felt that, faced with a similar situation, he would act in precisely the same way or perhaps with more violence than on that early morning when he refrained from doing anything irreparable. He just fled, fighting back his murderous inclinations, and wandered the streets waiting for daylight to lick the roofs, not knowing what to do or where to go, walking like a zombie through the freshly washed streets, not paying attention to the hostile glances of passersby, hastening to get nowhere, wanting to go north towards the Champs Elysées section to watch, like many other times, as the service entrance to the Paz residence flung open to let in the baker boy bringing fresh buns for the breakfast of the señores. Against his wishes, and to avoid being betrayed by his feet and walked to Blanca's despite the opposition of the rest of his body, he slumped down on the curb, hugged his knees and hung his head like a beggar so no one would recognize him. And back he went over his obsessions: setting, plot, alternatives, still feeling Blanca as part of himself even though she was no longer close. He recalled once more his last conversation with her, analyzed the phrases, the tone of voice, the relative emphasis of each word. Perhaps the expression on her face might yield a clue. He would gladly settle for any explanation, something that would justify her behavior and ease the anguish of not knowing why. Maybe he had made a mistake. Perhaps he had not been discreet enough in his eagerness to see her. Who knows, perhaps his letters had tipped the husband off and so he did not dare to go to the office for fear that Paz would simply throw him out. But no, Paz had nothing to do with his wife's behavior, poor Señor Paz was very kind and knew nothing of his wife's affairs. Maybe Paz was angry because he had not gone to see him after getting out of prison. Well, he really had not gone to see anyone: neither his former German students, nor his old comrades; even his family had gotten only a telegram asking for money. The clatter of cars, the screeching of trams, the voices of paper boys made him get up. He detested this morning bustle and wanted to avoid coming to the attention of policemen who were patrolling the area and who would surely ask to see his identification. He determined that the best he could do now was to try to get his things, so he headed for Corbalán's house.

Pablo Corbalán greeted him coldly. He had been informed by someone who happened to see Antonio on the street, on the very day of his release, that he had been out for about a week, and was dismayed that Gallego had made no attempt to contact any of his comrades. The doorman had also told him that Gallego had stopped by on three different occasions. Corbalán further assumed that Antonio was secretly in touch with someone in the party since the visit coincided with his expulsion, decreed the previous afternoon in an emergency session. They had charged Gallego with treason, with detailing names and places that had now been thoroughly raided. As dispassionately as he might report the weather patterns of Europe over the next forty-eight hours, and never giving him a chance to defend himself, Corbalán blanketed him with blame. And when Gallego, desolate and defeated, rejected the accusations one by one, Corbalán merely shrugged his shoulders. The welts on his back, that Gallego showed as proof of the high price paid for remaining silent, made no dent in his skepticism.

"For your information, I didn't vote in favor of expelling you. I abstained. But don't for a second think I count you among our heroes."

These final words were underlined with a pitiless sneer, an expression similar to one Gallego recalled in his tormentors.

Gallego knew about Corbalán's ruthlessness, his icy detachment. He was aware of the deftness with which Corbalán defended his ideas, of his ability to make his point of view prevail by crushing the most talented adversaries with his savvy rhetoric. Gallego felt overpowered, unable to muster either the energy or the arguments necessary to prove his innocence. He envied Corbalán now just as he always had. Pablo was far shrewder and much more ambitious than he, who was still a dreamer of happy endings for himself and for his country, dreams which he passed around with the generosity of someone giving out hope.

He let Corbalán call him ungrateful... and indeed he was. He had not yet thanked him for having picked up his belongings from the boarding house—where no doubt they would have been searched by the police—, for having stored them after removing anything that would compromise him, such as his papers: two folders packed with essays, an unfinished novel, and a series of reflections on love dedicated to Blanca. Corbalán assured him that he, naturally, had not read any of it. He had merely burned the whole lot in the stove one evening. But Gallego was convinced he was not telling the truth. He assumed that Pablo had thoroughly examined all his writings because his smile was a shade too ironic when he brought up

Blanca, whom he had met through some common friends when Paz asked him to take over Gallego's column while he remained in prison.

Now, five years later, after reading in the *Diario de Venusia* the summary of Corbalán's new novel Antonio Gallego had proof that Corbalán had read his papers. The novel, entitled *Senseless Days*, denounced the lack of freedom under Luzón as it chronicled the lives of poor squatters who had fled the southern parched lands ruled by unscrupulous landowners. He rushed out to find the novel, bought it at the first bookstore he came across, devoured it in one sitting where no one could observe the expression on his face or hear his blasphemies.

The dedication page of the novel burnt his eyes like acid: «For Blanca Alvarado de Paz, with eternal gratitude.» He read it twenty, thirty times over, he played with the words looking for every possible meaning, all the connotations of «gratitude» and «eternal,» he weighed each conceivable hint of intimacy or love that they might suggest. Those words did not refer exclusively to the fact that she had lobbied with her husband to have the novel published by their company, the most prestigious in the country, in spite of the reprisals decreed by the Luzón government ever since Paz and his associates had refused to toe the official ideological line. Knowing Blanca he needed no other words to confirm her relationship with Corbalán, since any mortal would be eternally grateful to have possessed such a goddess.

«For Blanca Alvarado de Paz, with eternal gratitude.» No, it was not gratitude inspired by political affinities alone that led Corbalán to express it in such a public way. It was, above all, a feeling of pride, sheer petulant boasting which made him print the name of his lover/sponsor on the first page. Like a badge worn on the lapel of a tuxedo on formal occasions, her name was paraded before anyone who cared to look. There was no doubt that «gratitude» referred to certain favors granted. He could not conceive how Corbalán could be so small as to brag to his readers of his benefactress' dishonor, nor how Blanca, ever so enigmatic and exquisitely discreet, had allowed such blatant mention of her relationship with the young writer, who was becoming increasingly prominent in the intellectual circles of Calipso. The fact that Blanca had left him for Corbalán, which all of a sudden seemed brutally obvious, hurt him as much as seeing her name printed in the book of his former comrade in arms.

IV

For five years, and until that day, Antonio Gallego's life had been spent in Venusia, with his family, in apparent monotony and absolute anonymity. He had become thoroughly distanced from militant politics, had made no attempts to vindicate himself and clear his name, had even avoided running into his former fellow students with whom he had formed one of the first revolutionary cells before leaving for Calipso to finish his liberal arts degree. Nevertheless, he continued to be virulently anti-Luzón even though, through family influence, his ideas were becoming more moderate. Almost every afternoon he accompanied his father to the gatherings of his Radical Party cohorts, who seemed to be more ardently trying to kill time—with the help of plenty of cognac—than do away with the regime. But shortly after Doctor Gallego's death Antonio severed all ties with his father's friends, conscious that he was not cut out for sitting endless hours in smoke-filled rooms. Therefore, in very polite if slightly condescending terms, he "declined the honor of being inducted into the Radical Party in order to continue his father's commendable work," as he had been invited to do by a distinguished group of local politicians who were at least twice his age. Not even the lure of being named their candidate for parliament as soon as Luzón's government fell, offered to him personally by the secretary general, could induce him to change his mind. He was flattered by the visit of the mythical Gumersindo Fontán, three-time presidential candidate, who came all the way from Calipso for the sole purpose of praying at the grave of his old friend the doctor, and to invite his son to fight for the cause of the Radical Party. Gallego did not need to give it a second thought. He argued that his time was taken up with managing the farm at Trebujar, the only source of family income now, watching over his mother's failing health, and working on his translations. He stayed away even in periods of euphoria, such as the winter of '52 when Luzón's fall seemed imminent and opposition forces were frantically meeting, debating, trying to come up with a joint program for peace. He also failed to attend the public festivities when the dictator did fall. He kept strictly to Trebujar where he spent all his time after getting a leave of absence for reasons of his mother's health from the Iberoamerican Publishing Company, where he had been a staff writer.

Señora Gallego was already over seventy. The years and progressive arteriosclerosis had ravaged her once distinguished beauty as well as her sharp mind. Sometimes she had no idea of who her children were and took Antonio for her father and Constanza for a maiden aunt who lived with them when she was a child. At other times she did not recognize Constanza at all and treated Antonio like a baby. She would cry and wail when she realized she could not cradle him in her arms. She would argue that he had been bitten by some tropical bug while he slept in his crib and had been turned into a prematurely aged monster. No one could persuade her that Antonio's six foot frame was the result of normal development; even though it was true that, as a child, he had been attacked by a swarm of bees, his growth was not due to poisonous stings but to perfectly natural physiological causes. It seemed clear that Señora Gallego had skipped over the last thirty-two years and gone back to the time right after the birth of her son, finally a boy after two girls and three miscarriages. This was the only plausible explanation for her constant fretting over whether Olvido Recasens, the wet nurse, was properly feeding the baby. There were moments when Doña Manuela's illness turned simply grotesque such as once when she demanded that Olvido breastfeed Antonio in her presence in order to check if he was getting enough milk or needed some additional formula. When people attempted to distract her from this enterprise, she threw an appalling tantrum repeating that her baby would starve to death from such neglect. One afternoon she was more violent than usual and managed to rip off the buttons of the servant's blouse. This scene disturbed everyone, particularly Olvido, who had been with the family since 1927 when she was hired as a wet nurse. It made Gallego suspect that Doña Manuela's obsessive maternal regression was in some ways the product of her own unconscious mind. Before losing her faculties she often anticipated doting on her grandchildren during her old age. But the married daughter who lived in Europe and could give her legal descendants, did not seem very inclined to humor her wishes. Constanza was single and past the marrying age. And, after he got out of prison, Antonio had broken up with that older woman, the one she had never liked very much because she feared she might not bear healthy grandchildren. Here in Venusia Antonio had not really been interested in any woman as far as she knew, and she would have been the first to find out given her many friends. There was no doubt that Señora Gallego, despite her delicate manners, had been a domineering woman who had wielded her power from behind the scenes and with so much tact that those around her had scarcely noticed. By means of kisses and caresses she had had more say than her husband in shaping and controlling the children. This made her deteriorating mental condition all the more painful, a most ironic twist of fate. Had it not been for the care given her by the children and Olvido, who had gone from nanny to nurse, someone might have confused her with one of the beggars who every Thursday came to the gate of Trebujar for alms. Seeing her usual unkempt appearance now, no one would suspect that in her youth she had been one of the best-dressed women in town, a real trendsetter thanks to her familiarity with French magazines that the owner of the leading Venusia bookstore imported from Paris especially for her.

Antonio Gallego felt infinite compassion for Doña Manuela but had a hard time still considering her his mother. It seemed to him that she had died a long time before, around 1952, just a few months after his father, when her blood began to lose its way to her brain. Feeling guilty, he suspected that he would only recover her after she was dead and buried, when he could forever substitute the current shattered image with the one he remembered from his childhood: the mother whose mere voice could chase away the terrors of the dark, whose only presence made things feel cozy once more. He had to constantly refer to his memories to find in the empty eyes of the old woman her former gaze, in which he had so often sought solace as an adolescent and even later. She could, without questions or resentment of any kind, share the void left in him by other eyes, a void that nothing else could fill.

It was on one of those difficult days when his mother was wandering aimlessly through the house that he picked up *Senseless Days*. His reaction was immediate: he set to writing a long critique of the text, a monograph to demonstrate that it had been plagiarized. Not only had Corbalán lifted the theme directly from Gallego's novel, but he had closely copied the style of a lesser known *indigenista* writer, Gabriel Martínez, whose work Antonio had studied in college. In fact, Corbalán must still have his copy of Martínez's best novel, *The Roots of the Myrrh Tree*, which he had lent him one night when they got to talking about literature after a political meeting.

In the afternoons, Gallego would often go to his room and lock himself away from the family's tragedy, lower the blinds as if to nap and proceed to work feverishly to prove Corbalán's guilt. Many of his evenings were devoted to this project as well. He gave up the Goethe translations on which he had labored steadily since his return home, and which had been his intellectual mainstay. Goethe, the writer he most admired among the classics, generously rewarded him. His works offered Gallego the opportunity to practice German, his second language, and to explore the master's fascinating personality. Antonio felt a certain affinity to the mature Goethe, the one who became a chronicler of his own life and wrote down minute and orderly observations about everything that went on. Just like Goethe, he kept close tabs on his own œuvre, classifying it in different black-covered folders. Gallego preferred square-lined paper because the diminutive spaces were perfectly suited to his almost microscopic handwriting, so hard to decipher at a glance. But it was not heartening to be like Goethe only in his passion for order and method, traits that to some degree he shared with many others. Gallego was intrigued by Goethe's genius, by his ability to discipline his spirit, and above all, by the fact that he sought to live a harmonious life. Antonio was positive that Goethe disapproved of Romanticism, that he rejected everything strident, exacerbated, morbid, anything that favored disorder. Although he was the author of *Werther*, after the trip to Italy Goethe's work stayed well within the parameters of Classicism.

He concurred with Goethe that the classics were the only models worth imitating, since their concept of art was based on harmony, objectivity, rigor, and health. Gallego hoped that by knowing and translating Goethe he could exorcise the demons lurking under his skin which still occasionally led him to identify with Werther, even though Blanca was nothing like either the fictive Charlotte or the real Charlotte Kestner, and much less like Friederike Brion, a character that had instantly fueled her fancy. The domestic ideal that both characters projected, namely a tranquil and almost dull kind of happiness, had little to do with Blanca's animal magnetism and his danger-fraught relationship with her. In any case, it was not *Werther* that he was translating but rather *Poetry and Truth*, Goethe's memoirs that had not yet been published in Itálica. He was particularly interested in how Goethe's life experiences had found their way into his work. While translating, Gallego kept detailed notes of his impressions that would serve, in abridged versions, as editorial footnotes. For instance, he commented at length on a passage from Volume III, Book IX, in which Goethe is galloping towards Drusenheim after having bid a final farewell to Friederike Brion. Suddenly his path crosses that of another rider and he is aghast to notice an identical horse, the same coat with gold buttons, and his own, if slightly aged, face. Eight years later, when traveling back to Sesenheim to pay a courtesy call on the Brion family he realized, at the exact spot, that he was wearing the same clothes as that long-ago rider. Goethe abandoned Friederike and everything she stood for: security, steady affection, the quiet contentment of country life, to go in search of his own destiny, convinced that he would not be swayed by feelings or even by the knowledge that he was "hurting the tenderest of hearts." Barely a few kilometers up the road the lovely young woman cried disconsolate, virginal tears. It would have been enough to tug a bit at the horse's rein, making it take him back, to dissipate that image which would haunt him until his death.

Gallego also became engrossed in anything that had to do with young Goethe's love life, perhaps because fate seemed to have a heavy hand in his affairs. A prime example occurred when Lucinda, the daughter of his dance teacher, fell in love with Goethe. Knowing it was a hopeless cause, and convinced of her powers, she put a curse on the first woman who let herself be kissed by the lips she had tasted. Maybe that was the reason—Gallego concluded—why Goethe inserted the travel anecdote into *Poetry and Truth* just one chapter before he told of his encounter with Friederike Brion. It was a way of predisposing the reader, of avoiding excessively harsh judgments, as if fate and not his own behavior had caused Friederike's suffering. Nevertheless, fate was not totally unkind to the young woman who, in the long run, got an acceptable part to play. The break-up with Goethe preserved her, in his memory, from the devaluation of what is familiar, from aging and decrepitude. By leaving him, Blanca too had made it possible for him to shield the image of her beauty from the ravages of time.

On occasion he found Goethe's behavior deplorable; Gallego detested his frivolity, his vampire-like talent for sucking out the best blood, the cleverest ideas and transforming them into some sort of magic brew with which to feed his imagination. However, Gallego was captivated by the ease with which Goethe triumphed, by his unswerving determination to write regardless of any and all obstacles. He was awed by the way Goethe ingeniously came up with the most appropriate disguise for each unique situation. As an aside to his own story of going to see the pastor of Sesenheim with Wieland while dressed in the tattered rags of a poor student, Goethe recalls in his memoirs that the gods always wore costumes when visiting the earth. Later, perhaps because one mask often leads to another, Goethe changed those clothes for the garb of a country rustic in his Sunday best. He liked to woo Friederike pretending to be somebody else, for instance a laborer on whom she could bestow her favors from her position of superiority. It was a game in which Goethe always won, even though it scared him because he knew himself to be cursed. Perhaps in an attempt to fool fate he tried to be taken for another man, even though it diminished his chances for success. When his lips brushed Friederike's skin, Goethe realized that he could not go on pretending. Still, the ploy allowed him to assert himself before the girl's laughing blue eyes that sparkled with the fullness of high noon. If he had kept his disguise, he might have broken Lucinda's magic spell. Friederike would have kissed the lips of a humble theology student dressed up as a bumbling country rustic, rather than those of the son of a wealthy Frankfurt family destined for glory.

Goethe's delight in costumes, masks, doubles, evident in *Poetry and Truth*, led Gallego to believe that this was a motif of great importance in his work. This was fully confirmed in *Wilhelm Meister* where the Count is shocked at running into his double, and by the strange resemblance between the countess and her sister Natalie as well as between her and her aunt. It was as if, through these fortuitous coincidences, Goethe wished to demonstrate that behind life's seeming incoherence there lay a deeper sense, that nothing was the product of chance but, rather, of the necessity of chance to fulfill itself.

Gallego immersed himself in Goethe, translating tirelessly. He felt encouraged by the support of his family, especially his father who was hoping that such systematic endeavors, for which Antonio had obvious talent, would help him overcome the depression into which he had sunk the first months after getting out of prison. Almost every evening, when the political chatter of the doctor and his friends began to wane, when street lamps came on, Antonio Gallego returned to his room to translate instead of going out to look for women or friends. It took him nearly three years to finish his version of *Poetry and Truth*. He offered it to the literary editor of the Iberoamerican Publishing Company, where he went each morning to warm his chair alongside other writers engaged in compiling entries for a medical encyclopedia. He pushed for the manuscript's publication, attributing the work to a good friend who, for political reasons, was exiled in Venezuela. Thus, in an attempt to avoid personal vendettas, Antonio Gallego hit upon Justino Ramírez as a pseudonym. The lengthy introduction to the text, as well as the footnotes, offered a rather unorthodox interpretation of Goethe. Gallego derived a great deal of satisfaction from the reviews, when more than one critic praised the impeccable translation or the provocative reading suggested by Ramírez. He chuckled to himself when the publisher thanked him for having brought such an excellent work to their attention. Gallego was gratified and mentioned the possibility of asking Ramírez to translate *Conversations with Eckermann*.

Approaching Goethe through the morose prose of his faithful companion excited him. That would put his skills to the test, challenging him to capture, and consistently reflect, the differences in style between Goethe and Eckermann. He finished *Conversations* in under a year and then, taking Eckermann as a point of departure, added some introductory remarks about the role of the go-between. One March morning, a few days before his father's death, Gallego gave the manuscript he had supposedly received from Ramírez to the director of the Iberoamerican Publishing Company. *Conversations with Eckermann*, which the publishers did not expect to do as well as the memoirs, came out a year later during the period of euphoria after the fall of Luzón. Possibly for that reason, it received little notice. Only the cultural pages of the *Diario de Venusia*, precisely in the same issue that weighed the impact of *Senseless Days* in the political life of Itálica, printed a brief but complimentary note. Therefore, it came as quite a surprise to Gallego when it was awarded the National Prize for Translation granted by the new democratic government. He went to Calipso representing Ramírez, to pick up a silver statue and a check for one hundred thousand pesos. The Undersecretary of Culture carried on, with the flowery language that the situation demanded, about the merits of Justino Ramírez, an intellectual who had chosen exile over life under a dictatorship. Gallego experienced an attack of radical self-disgust, as if suddenly his innards had burst and pus was oozing from every pore in his body. He would have gladly donated the prize money—which could only be collected by Justino Ramírez, in any case—to make Ramírez disappear, to never have invented him, or at least to have the nerve to destroy him right then, in front of everyone. But he did not dare to confess to the public that Ramírez was a pseudonym, that there never was an exiled Italican writer by that name, that the whole scheme had been the result of his pathological shyness. And the reason that he did not dare was that Pablo Corbalán, recently returned from Europe and hailed both as a hero and a consecrated writer, was sitting in the place of honor and stared at him with a spark of derisive skepticism.

When the ceremony was over Antonio Gallego dashed out of the building without greeting anyone, as if his worst enemy was giving him chase wielding a lethal weapon; he elbowed his way to the door as if he mistook the intellectual elite gathered there—the most distinguished members of the Italican intelligentsia—for a mob of subway riders during rush hour.

V

He slinks rapidly along Calipso's resplendent night, moving with long strides through the neon glitter. He hastens towards the darkness of his Trebujar, the black country night that does not harbor false sparkles, bare night stripped even of itself. But it is not a simple case of urban phobia, of distaste for a city adorned like a pagan whore ready to participate in a sacred rite. No. There are other reasons for his flight. He flees because only distance will help dispel certain images that will dissolve when his eyes can rest once more on familiar faces, on his everyday things. At times eyes the same color as his pursue him from a faceless void. At others he is chased by an enormous peacock with fanned-out tail and wearing a laurel wreath who tries to attack him—he feels like a kid at a costume party where a wicked, much older boy is bullying him. A peacock whose face shows a disturbing similarity to Corbalán's, whose body he might have inhabited in a former life.

He rushes through the wide streets seeking the nearest subway entrance in an attempt to make it to the north station in time for the last train to Venusia, since he is certain that the last flight took off two hours ago and that there is no chance of finding a bus at this hour. He checks his watch. If he could only catch the subway right this minute he might just have enough time. He will probably have to buy his ticket on board but he would not mind paying double the fare to get to Venusia tonight. He shudders at the thought of having to stay in Calipso, not out of any dislike for sleeping in a strange bed but because he is afraid of running into Corbalán somewhere.

The subway doors clanked shut right in his face. He had no choice but to wait around, anxiously pacing the platform. If the next train was running late it would make no sense to bother. He would take a taxi to the Hotel Honoris, an unassuming place in the old town, and get the first plane out in the morning. He tried to think about the things at hand and forget about himself. Deep down he considered his hatred of Corbalán sheer self-hatred. Thanks to Goethe he was learning to control his rashness; otherwise he might finally give in to the tantalizing lure of self-destruction and instead of boarding the train he would throw himself under it, to feel the coldness of the rails against his forehead. But he was too much of a coward even for that. He tried to deceive himself by arguing that his death would leave his family without protection and for their sake he must resist all such suicidal impulses. He wondered why he had not proclaimed his authorship of the translations after spending five years of his life hunched over pages by Goethe and by Eckermann. But what on earth for? No one would have believed him. Everybody, and particularly Corbalán who sat there like the pope ready to judge and condemn him, would have thought he was lying. He did, however, have ways to document his work, rough drafts of earlier versions, receipts for books ordered from Germany through his friend the dealer who would probably not mind testifying on his behalf. He could, if necessary, prove that Justino Ramírez never existed. He might even place an ad in the main newspapers of Venezuela requesting information about the exiled Italican writer and Goethe scholar, which no one would be able to answer. He wanted to be immediately acknowledged as the translator. Perhaps because, for a few brief moments, he had wished to become that peacock that he so fervently despised. He could safely assume that if Corbalán did not exist, or if he had not been presiding over the ceremony, he would have returned happily to Venusia, thrilled both with the success of his work and with his anonymity. But Pablo's presence had markedly unsettled him. Gallego knew him to be a plagiarist and felt nothing but contempt for his snobbery. Still he envied Corbalán. He envied his conspicuous self-satisfaction, his carefree nonchalance, the hard and mocking look in his eyes. But above all he envied Corbalán because he had never ceased to be himself. Instead, he had appropriated parts of others, of Martínez, of Gallego, always the best parts. First Corbalán stole the newspaper column, then he took the theme of his novel, and finally—Gallego had little doubt left—he robbed him of Blanca. Corbalán knew exactly what he wanted to become and was willing to face the challenge. He, on the other hand, would not take any chances. Therefore, he chose to deflect potentially hurtful comments and avoid any hint of disdain towards himself that might expose his extreme vulnerability. Just like a squeamish Victorian lady who, instead of doing needlepoint, takes to writing novels under an assumed name, pre-empting the possibility of receiving any sort of public recognition.

He glanced at his watch once more. There was no way now that he could make it to the train station. He climbed the stairs and walked out onto the former Luzón Boulevard now called Libertad. He crossed the street to get a taxi at the stand next to the Gran Hotel Itálica. It was an art nouveau building designed by several Catalan architects, a faithful follower of Gaudí among them, who imitated the façade of the famous Pedrera in Barcelona. The gardens were heavily Baroque, evoking the ocean bottom with tiles and mosaics in many different shades. He knew the place well because, as a child, he had stayed there on occasional trips to Calipso with his parents. As he passed the main door he looked inside almost instinctively, and there was Corbalán. He tried to avert his eyes but it was too late. Pablo, wearing a most disarming smile, was coming towards him with his hand outstretched. Gallego froze, incapable of walking off and leaving Corbalán standing there like a traffic cop in action. In the end he offered his hand and accepted the shake silently.

"I was looking forward to greeting you, but by the time I got a chance you had already slipped out. These massive events are quite bothersome, don't you agree? One is forced to speak with all sorts of bores. How are you? How's everything going? I've asked about you often but no one could tell me very much... All I know is that you left Calipso and are living in Venusia... By the way, I'm sorry about your father, please accept my sympathy. But let's go on in. I was looking for a friend, a French diplomat who is staying here. Give me just a minute to say my farewells, he leaves early tomorrow... Anyhow, congratulations, I'm very glad for you. I'm positive that you... But let's have dinner together, OK? Just excuse me for a second..."

Gallego listened to the friendly chatter without saying a word. He was not up to interrupting him, to inventing some excuse in order to walk out. He even acquiesced to dinner. Corbalán must have assumed that he was the translator, because otherwise why congratulate him. The need to assert himself before Corbalán, to show him that he was much more the intellectual, to force him to admit to his plagiarism in *Senseless Days*, to have him acknowledge that he had stolen the idea of presenting the corruption of the Luzón regime through a collective protagonist, made Gallego follow him into the lobby of the hotel. He let himself be introduced to the French diplomat as the person who had just received the National Prize for Translation.

They stepped outside. Gallego stated that he hardly ever visited Calipso and therefore knew only the places where he had gone during his student days: the old taverns, the downtown coffee shops, some cheap eateries in the port area. Corbalán insisted on taking him to a fancy restaurant, his treat of course, to celebrate their meeting. He knew just the place to feast, the La Marquise, and remarked that a content stomach was always a help for the muses. Writers should always guard themselves against indigestion, the result of poorly cooked gruel made with inferior ingredients. Eating well was one of the things he had learned while in exile, but it was through no particular merit of his. After all, he had been in Paris.

"No one can live in Paris for a whole year and not notice that French cuisine is by far the best in the world."

He had been enthralled reading *The Dictionary of Cooking* by Alexandre Dumas and by Brillat-Savarin's *The Physiology of Taste*, two jewels that he had picked up at the bookstalls of the *rive gauche de la Seine*. He pronounced these last words reverentially in French, as if it were a tribute to the language. Yes, in Paris he had discovered the pleasures of eating, something almost unknown or unpracticed in Itálica. "Even in houses where there is a certain culinary tradition, such as the Paz's, for instance," he added with a smile of complicity, "food just doesn't get the attention it deserves."

"Just to give you an idea of how much more civilized Europe is, there's the story about the Congress of Vienna in 1815 when the Czar visited Talleyrand's palace and insisted on seeing the kitchen. Naturally when they saw the Czar all the servants—waiters, cooks, dishwashers—promptly uncovered their heads and bowed. All of them, except the one wearing the tallest hat. 'Who is this man who dares to act so impudently?' demanded Peter, ready to unleash his wrath. 'He is the Head Chef, Sir,' replied Talleyrand solemnly. Remember, Antonio, that chefs always dress in white, like the pope, and wear headgear to signify their rank."

Gallego listens silently to the flow of conversation from Corbalán, taking note of his worldly sophistication. He would like to point out that while Corbalán was in Paris enjoying his golden exile many Italican farm workers were starving to death.

"Every emperor of a Western nation has bowed before the authority of the church. It's nice to know that at least once a czar had to come to terms with the fact that cooking is an institution perhaps not as powerful as the church, but much more... pleasurable... And popes have always been notorious gourmets. Why else should they insist on dining alone? So they can stuff themselves to their heart's content with abundant and exquisite concoctions! But, going back to what I was saying before, the Czar hired Talleyrand's chef, the great Carême, an exceptional man, an artist, much more Proustian than Proust since he sought to know the world, and offer it to others, through the sense of taste. His creativity and savoir faire were such that once he served a salmon decorated with roses and violets sprinkled with white wine from Alsace, and he had an assistant place the flowers around the fish so that they would look freshly cut, as if still showing traces of morning dew."

They arrive at a fashionable restaurant downtown. The maître greets them solicitously, bowing before Corbalán, expressing his gratitude to him for having chosen his dining establishment once more. Now he'll say again that I just got the National Prize for Translation. Getting it does not necessarily mean winning it. I should not let it upset me. After all, it's true that I just got it for someone else who happens to be me. But Corbalán doesn't introduce him. He just smiles condescendingly at the enthusiastic welcome and allows the maître to lead them to the best table, reserved for distinguished clients like them.

Antonio Gallego cannot explain why he has consented to all of Corbalán's suggestions when only half an hour earlier he was determined to escape from Calipso just to avoid such an encounter. Perhaps his urgency stemmed from a premonition that all of this would happen, that he would run into Corbalán and would be helpless to refuse his company. Now, sitting across from him eyeing the Sybaritic menu, Gallego makes up his mind that after dinner he will tell Corbalán once and for all what he thinks of him, everything that has been gnawing at him day after day. For the moment he just wants to gain some time and so he puts up with Corbalán's pedantic culinary digressions.

"If you want me to, I can recommend something... I know the menu quite well... French cuisine, as you can see... The *mousseline des fruits de mer*, or the goose... or the *paté à la velouté*... all of them are exquisite... As far as the main dish..."

"Thanks, I already know what I want. I don't dispute that French cooking is the best, I just happen to prefer our own. I'm not nearly as refined as you, but I will celebrate tonight. I'll have the salmon and a filet mignon. What do you think?"

The slight reticence in this final question does not escape Corbalán.

"This is a very nice place... you made a good choice. If it had been up to me we would have ended up in some noisy tavern eating meat and potatoes. Here it's so quiet that we can even hear our food."

Corbalán smiles. He is slowly sipping a scotch.

"I think you'll better understand my delight in food after you taste the appetizers. Besides, doesn't the most beautiful of the Platonic dialogues take place at a banquet?"

"Granted, but keep in mind that in *The Symposium* the focus was not the food but the conversation, the exchanges among the guests. The banquet was nothing but a ploy. And remember it was precisely Eryximachus who always urged people to eat and drink with moderation."

"I'm green with envy, Antonio. You have such a remarkable memory! The years are taking their harsh toll on mine... But I do recall, and this partly goes against your theory, that Aristophanes used food to illustrate androgyny... I think he compared the divided person to a flounder. He probably liked it *à la meunière*, don't you think?"

Gallego makes no reply. He is irked by Corbalán's tone, by his way of always having the last word. But he smiles to himself thinking that the remark about the flounder was a real boner.

"Your *mousseline* does look pretty good," comments Antonio while tasting his own appetizer totally oblivious to whether or not Corbalán agrees.

"Goethe was a gourmet, isn't that so?"

"Why should I know?"

"Well, it's common knowledge that you have read him very thoroughly, that you know his memoirs inside out. Right? Goethe always drank fine wines at family celebrations. And his wife, Christiane, was a terrific cook."

"Of course I've read him thoroughly, how else could I have translated him?"

"Aha! I should've guessed it. Did you go over Ramírez's drafts or did you two work together?"

Gallego does not answer. Instead he carefully chews his last bite of salmon.

"If I'm not mistaken you're fluent in German. You even translated some fragments of *Das Kapital* for us... wasn't it *Das Kapital*? Or maybe it was something by

Hegel? It's been so long... By the way, I suppose you heard that I was expelled from the party too, shortly after you were. In a way I had already left. The official line seemed to me thoroughly mistaken, almost inoperative. It was clear that they would never get to power."

"And that's about the only thing you care about: power."

"I admit I'm ambitious, why deny it? Power opens up possibilities, ways to solve problems, to help others, to change society... Only a more moderate left-center party had a chance to defeat Luzón and so I joined. We have to be realistic. That was around the time that I wrote *Senseless Days*. Have you read it?"

"Yes."

"Your eloquence might indicate that you didn't particularly care for it. Do you have the book?"

"Yes. I usually keep up with the new publications."

"I really would like to give you a signed copy. I guess I can still do it even if you already have one. After dinner we can stop by my place and have a drink. My apartment is not far."

Better wait until they are out in the street to tell Corbalán what he thinks of him, rather than make a scene here. In the meantime Gallego manages not to raise his voice but it takes all his self-control to suppress his rage and match Corbalán's impeccable manners. Anyone who did not know the details might think that his hatred for the man was not only groundless but also perfectly aberrant. Has Corbalán offended him by any chance? Has he humiliated him? Not at all, he has merely been witty in their far-ranging conversation. And Antonio has not been bad himself, actually keeping up rather nicely. But he must acknowledge Corbalán's superiority, based perhaps on a frivolous and caustic detachment that allows him to stay above everything. This, of course, implies that

Corbalán is familiar with places, things, experiences that others will not discover for years, if ever. That's what is so irritating, his incredible arrogance, concludes Antonio as he savors a piece of steak. Maybe Corbalán is a self-created genie; maybe one day he poured himself into a test tube and, after many a chemical reaction, emerged exactly as the person he wished to be.

"Have you been invited to the ceremony in honor of Humboldt?" asks Corbalán stirring him out of his reflections.

"No."

"I'll see what I can do. You might be interested in translating one of his pieces about Latin America. I'll speak to the secretary."

"Suit yourself."

"Humboldt was a great charmer. In fact, I'm preparing a lecture about him for the occasion... As I started to say, he was rather peculiar. Once, after returning from a trip, the king named him to the post of chamberlain. Humboldt confided to his friend Pictet that he was simply horrified to have people find out that he had merited such a ridiculous title. But perhaps you would like Armé Bonpland better. He accompanied Humboldt on his expedition to America and worked on gathering and classifying scores of plants, something like seventy thousand. Then, once back in Europe, he was unable to confirm Humboldt's conclusions and managed to write only four of the seventeen planned volumes about exotic plants."

"I'm very familiar with Bonpland's story. He happened to settle around Trebujar during his second trip. When his wife left him he took up with an Indian woman and filled the town with little creole kids. He died in absolute anonymity even though he could have been every bit as famous as Humboldt himself."

"And that is precisely why Bonpland envied Humboldt so, because he could never make good although he'd had similar possibilities."

"But then maybe he was happier than Humboldt who sought power and found fame," adds Gallego quickly siding with Bonpland before the Humboldt-Corbalán coalition. He swiftly calls for the check and insists on paying it over Corbalán's objections and reminders that he had chosen the place and should, therefore, be allowed both the consequences and the honor—he puts great emphasis on this word—of inviting him to dinner after such a long estrangement.

A taxi takes them along Libertad to the Plaza de la República. From there they make their way on foot through the narrow streets of the old city and stop in front of a solemn-looking house of austere classical lines, with four marble columns buttressing the façade. Gallego, loosened by the wine he drank during dinner, is ready to make clear why he did not care for *Senseless Days*, knowing full well that he will be violating the most elementary rules of hospitality. Corbalán ushers him into a small and sparsely decorated room.

"It's far from finished," he observes while turning on the lights. "I've only been here a few months and don't really plan to stay very long. I haven't made up my mind yet, but I've been suggested as ambassador to France. I know Paris quite well, have connections there, and that's always helpful. Besides, Paris is Paris..."

"By the way, I'd like Martínez's book back if you still have it. *The Roots of the Myrrh Tree*."

"Ahh, so it's yours! I knew it wasn't mine, but I couldn't figure out who had lent it to me. Of course, you were always interested in the *indigenistas*. Come, let's go into my study and see if we get lucky and find it."

As Corbalán searches the bookshelves Gallego sees a photograph of Blanca on his desk. He has seen it before because it is the same one she had given to him. This one has something written on the edge in Blanca's well-bred handwriting: «For Pablo, Blanca.»

When he notices that Antonio is looking at the picture, Pablo smiles in complicity.

"In a way, I met her thanks to you, when I took over your newspaper column. She asked me to pick up your luggage from the boarding house. She was afraid that the police would find something that would implicate her. She was in love with you at that time. But Blanca is quite changeable, you know how women are... The photograph was among your papers, you must have realized it was missing. I asked her to dedicate it to me. I also fell for Blanca. We became involved while I was her confidante. You will understand that I couldn't tell you the day you came to get your luggage, you were in no condition to hear about it then. Blanca had told me that you still loved her, that you might do something foolish to get her back. She swore me to silence. We were lovers for three years. Then, to tell you the truth, I got bored with the whole thing. But I still care for her, that's why her picture is on my desk."

"You're a bastard."

"Hey, don't take it so hard. She was pretty fickle herself. You weren't the first one..."

"You are a real son of a bitch. A goddamned manipulator. You seduced Blanca. You thought she might be useful. You copied my manuscripts. *Senseless Days* is plagiarized, the biggest farce in Italican literature. You didn't destroy my papers, you kept them and picked through them..."

"Shakespeare took his themes from minor authors without much talent. It's a well known fact that he plagiarized Marlowe..."

Antonio Gallego does not answer. He approaches the console as if to admire its delicate wood inlays. He picks up a set of keys, haphazardly left there perhaps, and holds them in his right hand. Then he slowly goes up to Corbalán, clenches his fist, and hits him in the face with as much force as he can muster. Corbalán stumbles against a bookcase and finally crumples to the floor. There is blood in his mouth and two of his teeth are broken.

VI

In the months that followed his encounter with Corbalán, Antonio Gallego often and vividly recalled the sensation of his closed fist hitting the jaw of the writer. That burst of violence was a liberating act that gave him strength, if not to start a brand new life, then to move on to a different stage where instead of letting himself be victimized by circumstances, he attempted to adapt them to his needs. He was no longer afraid of running into Corbalán because he knew that Pablo would never again look at him with disdain. On the contrary. Antonio assumed that, if anything, Pablo would now be the one doing the avoiding, wounded as he was not only in his pride but also in his vanity, with two front teeth missing. His only regret was not beating him up earlier, the day he went to get his things for instance, or even when it became clear that he had plagiarized his work, or when he read in the newspapers of Corbalán's triumphant return from exile.

The first step is to establish himself as the rightful translator and winner of the National Prize. He writes to the minister and encloses a stack of proofs, rough drafts of the translation, a receipt from the bookstore for the purchase of German texts, and even a letter from the director of the Iberoamerican Publishing Company confirming that Justino Ramírez is the pseudonym for Antonio Gallego.

Twenty days later the mail brings an answer. On behalf of the minister, the undersecretary reassures him that the evidence submitted will be carefully and impartially scrutinized by a committee of experts. Nevertheless, a most reliable source and personal friend, the writer Pablo

Corbalán, has stated that he is acquainted with an Italican exile named Justino Ramírez whose whereabouts are at this time unknown.

Gallego writes once more, in a blunt if consciously measured style meant to hide his outrage at Corbalán and this latest trick of his. Pablo has outdone himself as usual. There's no denying that. He has always managed to stay way ahead of the competition. He is such a bastard, this guy, a mother-fucking son of a bitch. Expletives float through his head as he tries to compose the letter which must show his determination both to clarify this matter and not to be intimidated by the lies of the soon-to-be ambassador. Therefore he requests that Ramírez's life be investigated, since the information offered by Corbalán must be purely coincidental. Justino was a name frequently heard in Itálica, especially in Venusia, where many families had named their sons after the foremost leader of the independence movement, Justino Caturales. As for Ramírez, it was a downright common last name. Gallego, however, fails to give a satisfactory answer to the final question posed by the undersecretary just before closing with «may fate protect you and reason be your guide» which has substituted the old formula employed until the fall of the Luzón regime: «May God grant you many years.» He fails because he really does not know his own motives except, perhaps, the desire to assert himself before Corbalán. Why else is he taking such trouble to be acknowledged as the translator and winner of the prize, when he had previously put so much effort into keeping his name a secret? Is it because of the money that he cannot collect otherwise? The people in the ministry want to know. No, he does not care about the money, he is not driven by material interest. There are personal reasons for his behavior and they are difficult to explain.

That letter is never answered. He writes once more
and his inquiry is again ignored. He goes to Calipso and
asks to see the minister. He is told that the minister has
nothing to do with his case and he better speak with
Undersecretary Artigas who has been in charge of the investigation.

On a blistering December morning—almost forty de-
grees centigrade in the shade—Venancio Artigas receives
him in a finely appointed office where fans are busily
humming. The undersecretary is slumped in a chair behind his desk and, as he listens, he doodles on the palm of
his hand with a pencil. He assures Gallego with sweat-
soaked words that there is nothing to worry about, that
every possible step is being taken to uncover the truth,
that the case is proceeding according to regulations.
Exasperated, Gallego demands to know what regulations
he means. Artigas, barely stirring in the heat that moist-
ens his cheeks, urges him to trust in the government of
Patiño and in the good faith of his staff to carry out the
complete democratization of Itálica, so ravaged until just
recently by the Luzón dictatorship.

Gallego leaves the interview in utter despair. He as-
sumes that, in spite of the good damp words, no one in
the ministry has any interest in investigating his case, if it
has ever been opened at all. He is grateful, at least, that
Artigas did not bring up his friend Corbalán. Surrounded
by the enervating yellow monotony of the landscape that
slides past the window of the train taking him back to
Venusia, Gallego makes up his mind to switch strategies.
He will take his case directly to the press and demand that
his name, not Justino Ramírez's, appear on the cover of
the translations.

He gets some encouragement from Bienvenido
Morros, the literary editor of the Iberoamerican
Publishing Company who has known him for a long time

and feels a certain affection for him. But, coming from Morros, those kind words are no better than yawns. Gallego must check with the editorial committee, with the editor-in-chief, even with the promotions people. In fact, and despite being convinced that Antonio is the real translator, Morros would not recommend putting Gallego's name on the second edition of *Poetry and Truth*. After all, it was Justino Ramírez who won the prize and his name carries a lot of well-deserved prestige among the readers. As far as *Conversations with Eckermann*, the first edition is not yet sold out, so speaking of changes at this point is a waste of time.

Gallego visits all five Calipso newspapers and receives uneven treatment. They are not sure who would be interested in his case, which does not qualify as news even in Venusia, his own hometown. People have other things on their minds, particularly these days when it seems that the Patiño government intends to call for free elections next spring. Nevertheless, the *Diario de Venusia*, the most influential paper in the city, publishes a very nice picture of him in which the physical resemblance to Corbalán is apparent. The interview takes up two columns of the Thursday culture section. Gallego quotes the classics, wittily paraphrases the author of *El Lazarillo de Tormes* who also remained anonymous because, as Cicero put it, «honor makes for art»; that is, honor understood as fame. The desire for fame, deserved for one's own individual efforts rather than inherited from one's ancestors, has always moved men to action, especially some Renaissance humanists like the followers of Martin Luther or Erasmus of Rotterdam. Still, Gallego is very proud of his elders. Of his grandfather, the seaman who anchored in Calipso and stayed in Itálica for the rest of his life where he made a considerable fortune. Of his father, an eminent physician and avowed proponent of democracy. But Gallego feels that his intellectual endeavors, humble as they may be, have lifted him above his origins. That is why now he wants to forego anonymity and make his name known to the public, to have his accomplishments properly recognized. He compares himself to a captain who, having entered the enemy fortress, killed the guards, and opened the way for his troops, desires a medal and his name inscribed not necessarily in the already jammed pages of history but in those of the *Military Gazette*, and on a street of the town where he was born. But—Gallego continues drawing out his bellicose simile—he had no interest in being remembered if instead of victory he had led his troops into defeat. In a similar vein, he had been afraid that his work, the assault on the fortress of Goethe's œuvre with its treacherous access and its intricate web of tunnels and corridors, might end in failure. That is why he withheld his name, thus avoiding the enormous responsibility of translating the ultimate of classic texts, the words of the greatest genius in modern European literature. When asked if he planned to continue translating Goethe he answered negatively. He was currently at work on a monograph where he would document Corbalán's absolute lack of originality. The final statements, explaining why he considered Corbalán a plagiarist, are mangled in reproduction since Gallego went into much more detail than the newspaper was willing to print.

Interviews also appear in *La Tarde* and *La Verdad*, not in the culture section but in the local news, among the obituaries and the list of pharmacies open through the night. The headlines announce that Gallego is writing an essay on *Senseless Days*, but his statements about Corbalán are given short-shrift and criticized.

He sets aside the almost finished translation of *Wilhelm Meister*, reshelves the German dictionaries, puts away the Spanish and French versions that he regularly consults, stores the portrait of Goethe that presides over his desk, and devotes all his time to the piece on Corbalán. He minutely researches each and every one of the sources, even the most obvious ones, looking for similarities with the work of other authors whom Corbalán might have cribbed or paraphrased. Gallego devotes a full sixty pages to the story of how Corbalán came into the possession of his manuscript. The chapter reads like a detective novel and is appropriately entitled «The Case of the Stolen Trunk.» When he is certain that he has listed and thoroughly documented all the mistakes, references, borrowings of his enemy, he considers his work finished and calls it *Senseless Days: Portrait of a Plagiarist*.

It has been two years since he read in the *Diario de Venusia* the first review of Corbalán's novel. The Patiño government has seemingly forgotten its offer to hold free elections. From the Italican Embassy in Paris, Corbalán has announced a forthcoming book of essays. The Ministry of Culture has still not closed his case and has neglected to contact him to provide any update, the smallest explanation of the proceedings, or even to confirm that any of the promised investigations have been carried out.

When his leave of absence from the publishing company ended Gallego chose to give up his job rather than leave Trebujar. He did not need the money and Morros, who pleaded with him to resume his position as staff writer, did not deserve any sacrifices. He had managed only to have the editorial committee agree to insert a note on the inside cover of the second edition of Goethe's memoirs to the effect that Justino Ramírez was a pseudonym. As a result, Gallego wanted nothing to do with that rabble and did not even bring them his monograph for publication. He sent it instead to the most important Italican publishing houses in Venusia and

Calipso. «Your study is very stimulating but our publication schedule is set for the next year. Perhaps at some later date...» «We would publish it if that far-fetched story of the stolen trunk was omitted...» «It was about time for someone to tell the truth about Corbalán. However, we have just asked the government for a subvention and it would be counterproductive to publish such a libelous essay since Corbalán is on very good terms with the Minister of Culture.» «If you agreed to rewrite parts of it changing the tone...»

Gallego decided to publish the book just as he had written it, without cuts or alterations, without corrections or adjustments of any kind. He could well afford the luxury of paying for the publication himself. He did not wish to wait or compromise. He was afraid that if Patiño stayed in power sooner or later Corbalán would be named Prime Minister.

Olvido, the old family servant, had a son who worked as a typesetter. He occasionally came to Trebujar to visit his mother or take her home to help out, since he was a widower with small children. Each time Olvido saw Macario coming she would rush to ask permission to leave for a few days, because whenever her son needed her he never inquired if it was all right. He would simply act the kidnapper, lifting her in his arms and depositing her in the front seat of his truck without any ado such as changing clothes or packing. Gallego, who having nursed at the same breast felt a certain closeness to Macario, once asked him the reason for such odd behavior. He was told rather curtly that if Olvido, his mother, wished to continue being a slave to the family, he did not. If he could not sever her chains he could at least show the Gallegos, through his lack of consideration, that he was a free individual, that both his beliefs and his actions were those of a true revolutionary, something that middle-class people, even those who had been in prison, could never hope to be.

Antonio Gallego liked Macario and never took his eccentricities too seriously. He would, in fact, chuckle right in his face about the ferocity with which Macario defended his beliefs, about his image as the reformed tough now committed to serving the people's cause. So on one of Macario's visits, Antonio asked him if he would print his book. Macario's answer brimmed with irony. He began by stating that he was flattered by such a proposal. "This is quite an honor, coming from someone like you with so many connections in the publishing world. Besides, I have nothing to lose since I won't have to worry about sales." Gallego felt obliged to explain that ethical reasons prevented him from agreeing to the conditions imposed on him by other publishing firms. His main goal was to have the book come out just as he had written it. Macario, putting on airs as if he were the most selective editor in the whole country, said that he would like to take a look at the manuscript before making any decisions.

Two weeks later when Antonio dropped by the printing shop to check with Macario, he was shown several sets of samples in different type for him to choose. Macario had found the book very interesting since he, and others more knowledgeable in those matters, considered *Senseless Days* a testimonial for the oligarchy. The working class was depicted as a collective puppet controlled by the rich and, even though the novel had greatly contributed to the fall of Luzón, it had failed to capture the real feelings of the common folk. The people, Macario solemnly pronounced, were hungry for changes and not only in economic terms. They wanted justice. Only a bourgeois author could give such a slanted perspective.

The 1 500 copies of Gallego's essay were printed in just under three weeks. Macario himself oversaw the binding process and, when the very satisfied author asked for the bill, Macario said that he would only accept reimbursement for materials, not labor. Antonio insisted and they finally reached an agreement: Gallego would pay back in kind if the occasion ever arose.

Senseless Days: Portrait of a Plagiarist suffered from lack of publicity and poor distribution. Its publication went largely unnoticed by both the critics and the reading public, despite its provocative title intended to stir interest and controversy. Gallego waited in vain for some sort of reaction from literary magazines. The press barely mentioned it and only two newspapers, one in Calipso and one in Venusia, carried brief reviews. One judged it sensationalistic and vindictive, the result of a personal vendetta. It seemed written out of hatred which, like other strong feelings, clouds the mind and invalidates all conclusions. It ended with a radical dismissal that cut deeper than any other charges: «Barking dogs never stopped a caravan.» The other one appeared in Venusia's radical paper and concluded that the desire for public recognition had been the motivating factor behind the essay. The reviewer recalled how in a recent interview Gallego had revealed that Justino Ramírez was his pen name and he wanted everyone to know it. By contrast, he now claimed that Corbalán had passed himself as Antonio Gallego when he plundered the unfinished manuscript by the same title.

Meanwhile, bookstore windows displayed a volume of essays called *Lights and Shadows (About Baroque Poetry)*, authored by the Italican ambassador to Paris.

VII

The coup against Patiño took place around the time that Señora Gallego died. Once more, and for the twentieth time since Itálica became an independent nation, a faction of the armed forces revolted against those in power. Antonio Gallego followed the events with a certain aloofness as if he were an exile and Itálica only a haphazardly adopted country that would never become his true homeland. This attitude could be partly attributed to the trauma of his mother's death which, although wished for in the darkest hours, left him as helpless and lonely as a child. When he buried her, in the rural cemetery's only elaborate crypt, he did not bury his childhood as he had anticipated. It was as if the child he had been, and whom his mother so obsessively recalled during her last years, had come back to life and taken over his body and soul. The passage of time, the change of seasons, even his own body's physical rhythms, everything took on a different meaning, much more oriented towards the past than the future, back to the time of his infancy.

The emotional upheaval brought about by his mother's passing motivated him to write again. This time it was not in order to publish but rather to find himself, or what was left of him, lost amid his loathing for Corbalán, his shrinking self-esteem, and the dregs of his passion for Blanca.

He wrote his own story, setting down his feelings and intuitions to protect them from oblivion, to avoid having them swallowed up in time's wake. He wrote because he wanted to conjure up and chase away the monsters which plagued his reasoning, get rid of the specters that had haunted him since his early years, turning him into a weak and frightened person incapable of accepting himself. He sought to create a parallel, yet different, world through which to explain and understand the real one. He made the decision to populate it with characters that were very similar to the people in his life. Nothing was coincidental, everything was carefully controlled. Corbalán, Blanca, his family, all of them appeared in the pages that were piling up. They mirrored his obsessions and forced him to come to grips with them. Since he was so absorbed in what was happening in the pages that he was writing he barely paid attention to his country's political crisis, to the newspapers that reached Trebujar with great delay, or to the radio news broadcasts, interrupted frequently by military marches or classical music, that his sister listened to with the volume way down because she was still in mourning. But then Cardona, the next military leader and self-proclaimed President of the Republic, ordered five hundred farm workers massacred simply because they had naively assumed that the land should belong to those who worked it and had occupied some plots that were empty and unused. At that point Gallego swore to himself that he would do everything in his power to help oust Cardona, even though his sister thought that such a drastic measure had perhaps been necessary.

Trebujar was barely thirty kilometers away from where the events had unfolded. Ten days later his foreman informed him that arms and ammunition, which did not seem to belong to the army, had been found in a heavily wooded area of his property. Gallego chose not to call the police. Even though it was for his own protection, he abhorred the idea that the very people responsible for the massacre might show up on his farm.

Six months after Señora Gallego's death Olvido asked Constanza for permission to go stay with her son Macario. Since she was now not urgently needed at Trebujar she felt an obligation to help him. She did not rule out the possibility of coming back when the children had worn her out and, of course, she was counting on spending her last years with the Gallego family, where she knew she was guaranteed a wool blanket and a good mattress to do her dying. Antonio Gallego himself drove her to Macario's printing shop on the way to the Venusia railroad station to pick up his cousin Gabriela, who had just returned from Europe and was coming for a visit.

He saw her step off the train but did not immediately recognize her. She was the one who approached and kissed him with the same openness they had shared as children. She had on a red suit with a pleated skirt and a black tight-fitting top, and was carrying two heavy leather suitcases. He was rather surprised. He had expected her to wear mourning black and be much less attractive. On the way to Trebujar he realized that, just as when they were little, he would have a hard time being around her. Gabriela talked too much and had a tendency to correct others. She had come to take her cousins' minds off their recent loss and intended—she unabashedly admitted as much—to turn the house topsy-turvy. She wanted to socialize with other nearby landowners, and have fancy parties as soon as the period of mourning allowed. She had a beautiful voice, warm and full of cadences, and could carry a tune.

"Do you want me to sing something for you?"

"I had no idea that you liked to sing."

"Oh, I most certainly do. I'll sing you a tango."

She belted it out as if she were on stage: the drama, the gestures, the modulated subtlety. It wasn't half bad. Not at all.

"Applaud if you liked it, I'll hold the wheel."

Antonio Gallego compared Gabriela's presence to the aftermath of a hurricane, not so much for the damages she caused but for the restoring frenzy that ensued.

Trebujar changed drastically with her arrival. There were freshly planted flowers in the garden, the furniture was moved around regularly, and workmen were busy with the bathrooms, bringing them up to current hygienic standards, as she proclaimed with more than a tinge of irony. The neighbors could count on her visit at least once a week, even if she had to go on foot when occasionally Antonio refused to drive her and she could not find another willing chauffeur.

"What really bothers me," is the way Antonio's conversations with his sister usually began, "is not Gabriela's eagerness to organize everything which actually makes time pass and is helpful after all, since the bathrooms did need remodeling. No, it's the way she's always poking around my business. Ever since she came here I cannot concentrate. She knows that I'm busy writing and still barges into my room without knocking, reads over my shoulder and even ventures her opinions..."

He came near to moving to Venusia to see if, once there, he could recover his equanimity and write without interruptions, but his sister prevailed on him to stay. So he resigned himself to the situation. Gabriela had said that she was staying for two months, and one had already passed. Showing any signs of distress, let alone asking her to leave, was absolutely out of the question. Gabriela was their mother's beloved goddaughter, the flighty one in the family. Neither Swiss boarding schools nor the Aescolapian nuns of Calipso had managed to tame her. And, having been brought up to marry like all the girls of the upper class, Gabriela proclaimed that she would claw and bite her way out of any such arrangement, if it came to that. She did not like children and rejected the notion of family obligations; having to stomach the same one man day in and day out, she announced, would make her retch. She was delighted to be thirty already since, past that age, her chances of marrying were minimal and her mother would at last have to content herself with having a single daughter and would stop lecturing her on how to please her potential suitors. Her phobias notwithstanding, Gabriela was thrilled to be the focus of attention and the object of desire. Still, she would refuse the proposals of the would-be husbands in the same spirited manner in which she had welcomed their overtures.

"I love to be desired," she confessed to Antonio the day that he ventured to compliment her on her eyes, saying that they were about the prettiest ones he had ever seen. She was slightly miffed by the qualifier, and demanded to know just whose were the prettiest. Antonio Gallego declined to specify, evading the issue by saying they belonged to "the woman of my dreams." That very night Gabriela, barefoot to avoid being heard, sneaked into Antonio's room wearing a satin and lace nightgown.

"I am the woman of your dreams," she sighed nearing his bed only to peck him on the forehead and slip out again laughing before his bewildered eyes that looked as if he, indeed, was dreaming.

Two nights later it was Antonio who knocked on Gabriela's door. "Come in," she whispered and smilingly made room in her bed, as if she had been waiting. When dawn rudely began to scratch on the window panes and the lark sang in the garden, he returned to his room. He stayed awake, blissfully tired, until it was time for breakfast. He was savoring the taste of fresh kisses and warm skin that took him back to the days in Calipso. When he tried to compare these caresses with those others, the feel of Gabriela's body with Blanca's, he realized he could not. Both his memory and his senses were replete with the overwhelming physical presence of his cousin. He wished the time away, longed for the daylight hours to fly and night to lend its cover so that he could possess her once

more. He could never have anticipated that this bothersome relative would become so intensely magnetic for
him. Barely a week ago he would have given anything to
get rid of Gabriela and now he simply would not allow
her to leave under any circumstances. He wondered just
when it had all begun, because it was certainly long before
she surrendered to him, way before she came into his
room. It must have been about four days and a few hours
ago, he decided, completely at a loss to explain the whys
and wherefores, or to imagine her motives. He knew only
that, all of a sudden, in the garden where they had played
together as children on summer days, out there near the
fountain, he had looked at Gabriela and discovered himself flooded with an old forgotten feeling, something akin
to tenderness. And for the first time in years he felt in
tune with the landscape, with the people that surrounded
him and, most of all, with himself.

Every night as soon as he thought Constanza was
safely asleep, once the lights in the kitchen went out and
all the little domestic noises ceased, he would cross the
hall and steal into Gabriela's bedroom. Holding her close
he would feel his accumulated anguish melt as he put his
past into words—the words of a rescued shipwreck survivor talking into the night with a captain willing to listen to his story. When he would finally muffle the cries of
passion, the spasms of lovemaking against her cheeks or
her breasts, it seemed to him that all his previous experiences made sense only because they had brought him to
this place, to this body. He asked Gabriela to marry him, or
at least to swear that she would never leave Trebujar, but
she was noncommittal. And when he, inflamed with
jealousy, demanded to know why, she indicated that she
could not be sure just how long she would love him.

"I have no idea what I'll be doing next month, let
alone next year... How can I possibly promise you eternal

devotion? Besides, what if I met Corbalán and...," she added playfully as she kissed him. "Why do you want me to swear to something absurd? And that goes for you too. How can you assure me that you'll still be in love with me a year from now?"

Whenever Antonio got started professing his undying adoration, Gabriela would kiss him quiet and entreat him to love her right then and there.

However, with characteristic stubbornness Antonio Gallego kept harping on the need to get married, and questioning her reasons for refusing. Finally Gabriela stated the obvious: that this was not the first time she had been in love and that she could not swear to a faithfulness that, in principle, she did not believe in upholding. She did not wish to be forced, like on other occasions, to fake it, to continue kissing ardent lips with her cold ones, or to give her body reluctantly to another one that continued to claim it. When she was younger she thought herself capable of loving only one person all her life; she thought she would never tire of her first lover. But one day, shortly before the wedding, she became aware of the monotony of her fiancé's kisses, of the mechanical way in which he caressed her, of the predictability of his touch, of the repetitive nature of his whispered endearments, and she felt her arms grow heavy and eager to let go of a body that they never again wished to embrace. And there were no guarantees that it would not happen again. No, she was not the faithful kind. Maybe she did not know how to love. She had never learned. She just couldn't. She would try not to hurt him too much when she had no alternative but to leave him, when weariness set in, when the seemingly inexhaustible desire ran dry. But instead she promised to wait for him each night with her door unlocked until she stopped loving him. Only then would he find the bolt latched, and the next day she would leave

Trebujar without regrets or reproaches. Antonio agreed, praying that the moment would never come. He felt their mutual desire stoked rather than sated by lovemaking and hoped that this arrangement could go on indefinitely.

Gabriela wrote to her mother that she was staying a while longer. In Calipso the situation was downright alarming. Cardona's government, weakened by infighting, was resorting to repression in order to stay in power. The capital's newspapers, censored since the colonel took office, made only veiled references to arrests and tortures, to *desaparecidos*. The cities were patrolled by special units, para-military forces under the direct control of the Minister of the Interior, that committed the worst atrocities with absolute impunity. "We are living in sheer collective insecurity," Señora Orbajosa wrote to her daughter Gabriela. Just like me before the possibility of a locked door, muttered Antonio off-handedly. Gabriela picked up on the allusion at once, but it went by Constanza who was sometimes irritated by the antics of the couple, although she secretly appreciated being let in on them, and who did not remotely suspect that they spent their nights together.

One afternoon Macario drove up to the gate in his truck. He parked it and sauntered up the path to the house whistling. Without stopping to greet anyone he proceeded directly to the second-floor living room, where he knew the family would be gathered at that time having coffee. He wished them good health, as was his habit, and requested to speak briefly to Señor Gallego in private.

"It'll only take a second. I need to ask a favor of you."

"How's your mother doing? Tell her we miss her around here," put in Constanza before Gabriela's inquisitive gaze.

"Thank you. She's just fine. I'll give her your message. Good day."

Macario followed Gallego out of the room.

"It's not necessary to go to your study. I just came to ask for a special favor. I have a good friend who needs your help."

"What about?" asked Antonio, intrigued. "You know I have little influence around here and very few connections."

"I know, I know. But what he needs is simple and you can do it. He wants you to check some translations from the German. That's all."

"Consider it done. Tell him to come by anytime. I'll be glad to do it."

"That's the hitch. It's you who must come with me, and the sooner the better. I'd be much obliged."

"Is it that pressing?"

"Yes. Yes it is. I tried to come earlier this morning, but I just couldn't get away until now. Trust me."

133

VIII

Following Macario's rattling truck on the highway
from Trebujar to the outskirts south of Venusia, Antonio
Gallego wondered what could possibly have made the
typesetter seek him out so urgently. He guessed that it had
something to do with a job. Macario worked with young
writers eager to have their poems printed and willing to
pay for it. Antonio conjectured that maybe one of them
wanted to enrich his book with quotes from some
German poet. He recalled his own youthful enthusiasm
for Hölderlin and Novalis, which made him learn
German in order not to miss their slightest nuance
through someone else's faulty translation. Of course, he
could count on both the money and the encouragement of
his father, a man of learning who spoke several languages. This was likely not the case with Macario's friend
who was so eagerly requesting his help. However, when
he noticed that Macario bypassed the road that led to his
shop and instead turned onto a secondary one that paral-
leled the main route, he figured that the translation
probably had nothing to do with literature. Perhaps it was
some political communiqué or even a subversive pam-
phlet against the Cardona regime. But why in German?
Few Italians spoke or even understood it, although during World War II there had been a huge immigration of
German Jews who were fleeing the Nazis. Later on, with
Luzón's blessings, came the Nazis themselves, fleeing the
Allies. But neither group had the slightest desire to take
up a political fight. The first was busy establishing prosperous businesses or arranging to go to Israel; the second
tried, above all, to go unnoticed, leading impeccably
anonymous, sometimes even exemplary humanitarian
lives. Or perhaps Macario was involved in espionage and

his business was only a cover that gave him access to certain kinds of information... No, that was absurd. Macario only handled texts without much importance. Besides, what foreign power would hire crazy Macario even as a shoeshine boy for the least of its agents? Could it be drugs? A shipment of cocaine to be smuggled to Germany? Wasn't it repeated over and over that Itálica was the second largest exporter of that substance in Latin America?

Macario made a sharp right turn down an unpaved road. He drove up to a garbage dump and got out. A few hundred steps away stood the remains of a building and a stable. Everything seemed abandoned. Macario approached Señor Gallego's car and suggested that he wait there.

"It'll be just a second."

He was back out of the stable in less than five minutes. He had new orders.

"Roberto Manzanas is waiting for us at the Café Viena on Independencia Avenue. Do you know where that is?"

"Surely."

"I'll go on ahead. If we get separated when we reach downtown, we'll just meet there. OK?"

Antonio parked two blocks away from Independencia and walked the broad avenue towards the Viena amid the shrill squeaking of street cars and the hum of traffic. He had gotten used to Trebujar and now the city struck him as strange, particularly at that precise moment when the metallic light of the street lamps came on suddenly, without the least regard for the sun's final, colorful minutes, for the day coming to a close. He walked with big steps towards the cafe. He was anxious to get this over with and rush back home into Gabriela's arms.

Sitting in a booth at the Café Viena he could not avoid seeing the image of himself as a child in that same spot with his parents and sisters. They went there quite regularly on Sundays for their afternoon tea. A small musical group would fervently scratch waltzes, and a chubby and friendly waiter served them. They would order meringue-covered concoctions that his mother described one day, in a flight of lyricism, as "a boat carrying a cloud across a tranquil lake" in order to get him to stop poking at his pastry and eat it.

Macario had not arrived yet, and Gallego did not know Manzanas. It was still early. Macario should be there soon. He passed the time observing the faces of the pedestrians under the yellowish artificial light that turned the citizens of Venusia into hepatitis sufferers one and all. Most people were rushing as if they were late, their hands full of packages, baskets, bags, pocketbooks, cardboard boxes, balls. Not one person had a book. What an uneducated country, he thought to himself. Suddenly he saw a young girl approach carrying a book. As she passed by he made out the title: *Senseless Days*.

He ordered a cognac and a newspaper. He read the headlines. He looked at his watch once more. A young man came towards his table. He had on wirerimmed sunglasses, not the thing to wear at that hour of day, and he was neatly dressed.

"Señor Gallego? Macario asked me to come."

"Why is that? I thought he would come with you. Are you Manzanas?

"No. I'm here on behalf of the person you came to see."

"The persons. Macario was also supposed to be here. What will you have to drink?"

"Coffee, thank you."

"Well, you tell me."

"Pardon me for asking, Señor Gallego, but do you smoke?"

"I assume you didn't have me come here just to check that..."

The young man did not answer. He searched in his pocket and took out a pack of cigarettes that was crushed flat. He tried to put it back into some sort of recognizable shape. Then he stuck his finger into the opening and took out two cigarettes. He offered one to Gallego.

"Please."

"Not now, thank you."

"Please, do have one. You'll immediately see why."

He lit Gallego's cigarette and then his own. He started to play with the wrapper, spreading it out on the table as he sipped his coffee. After a pause, he asked Gallego to look down at the paper. It had a message in German, written in meticulous handwriting.

"Macario said you could be trusted. Please, would you translate this as literally as possible?"

"I have no idea what Macario said about me. But he certainly has not given me the slightest explanation about any of this and I think I deserve one..."

"It's much better for you to remain in the dark. Now, please tell me what it says but don't look as if you're reading."

Gallego conveyed the message.

"The weather will improve next week. It's better to wait because there is a chance of a storm from the east. Take out the umbrellas but don't open them yet."

"Are you positive that it says to take out the umbrellas or just to have them ready?"

"I think to take out is closer to *nehmen* than just to have them handy."

"Thank you, that's what I thought. Manzanas understood it as to have them ready. It's not the same. If it's going to rain, better to have them out and not stored away in the junk closet."

"Anything else?"

"No. We consulted you for your expertise in German. As you can see I know a little bit too. I've read your translations and they're superb. Macario told us that they're yours under a pseudonym. By the way, I know someone named Justino Ramírez. But don't worry, he's absolutely illiterate. Thank you very much. You'll forgive me if I don't explain any further."

"I'll settle it with Macario. I really would like to know who in the world you are."

"I'm very sorry, sir, but I'm not authorized to reveal anything."

The man tore up the paper into tiny bits and placed them in the ashtray where he proceeded to put out his cigarette. Then he got up.

"We better not leave together. Please stay here a few minutes while I make my exit."

He went up to the bar, paid the check, left, and got lost in the crowd. Gallego still waited a while before he went to get his car.

IX

Two weeks after that encounter Amparo, the foreman's wife, gave Señor Gallego an unstamped envelope
that had apparently been mysteriously delivered to the
farm. They had found it by the garden gate, where someone must have left it. It was thickly stuffed and had
nothing written on it except the addressee's name in capital letters. Antonio Gallego opened it at once. Two sheets
of white bond folded in quarters covered a small strip of
paper with a typed message:

Thursday at seven the master will see you at
the Viena to continue your lessons. Please
acknowledge receipt and send your answer.

There was no doubt. The mysterious sender was
Macario who probably wanted him to translate another
coded communiqué. That's what the lessons must refer to,
and the master must be the young man with the dark
glasses or perhaps Manzanas himself. As far as acknowl-
edging receipt and giving an answer, how was he supposed to do it if they did not give any indications?

He mentioned it to Gabriela and Constanza at lunch,
and neither of them seemed thrilled by the prospect.

"Don't you think it's risky?" Gabriela asked in an ex-
ceedingly intimate tone.

"Of course it's risky. Macario is really reckless. Who
knows, he might even be a member of AVE, the group
which claimed responsibility for planting the bombs that
went off at the military headquarters in Calipso."

"I don't think so. Macario a member of AVE? Not a
chance!"

Gabriela's voice was much deeper than Constanza's
and she spoke more slowly. Antonio liked to hear her

even when he wasn't listening, when she chatted about domestic matters with Constanza while he pretended to read. That daytime voice evoked the other one, the one he preferred, when during lovemaking Gabriela's liquid moans reminded him of all the sounds of the sea. His sister's voice, on the contrary, was sharp, almost piercing. It echoed her fears and apprehensions, and gave audible proof that Constanza was forever on the lookout for dangers, always anticipating accidents. He was delighted by Gabriela's concern but found his sister's warnings absolutely unfounded.

"That's all we need, for you to be thrown back in jail. Have you forgotten how awful it was?"

"That won't happen this time. I have nothing to do with politics... But let me tell you, the situation is so bad that I feel like planting some bombs myself."

"Constanza is right. Before I came to Trebujar the police had picked up more than six hundred people in Calipso alone. In her last letter Mother writes that the number is now around three thousand. The university is closed and there are no immediate plans to reopen it."

"With the excuse of a curriculum change, just like in the time of Luzón. Remember?"

They were having dessert. The maid told Señor Gallego that the foreman would like a moment with him after he finished eating, if possible.

"Have him come up, we're almost done."

As usual when he spoke to the Señor, Natividad held his cap in his hand. The cap was his good luck charm, and according to his wife he wore it even in his sleep. He did not know how to do anything without it, nothing at all, she joked.

"I wanted to ask permission to order twenty doses of artificial insemination from the vet. Forgive me, ladies..."

"I thought I had already told you to go ahead."

"But I've reduced the quantity. I had talked with the administrator about getting forty."

"Well, consult with him in that case."

"He left for Venusia this morning and won't be back until Saturday, sir. If you have any business in town, perhaps you might convince him. I personally think that our bulls are powerful enough to... forgive me, ladies... we don't really need to inseminate."

"We already discussed that and decided to try insemination this year. I was under the impression that you agreed..."

"Yes, sir. Whatever you say, sir. But if you accept this change the administrator won't get his way. I would like to try just with half the cows... get only twenty doses instead of forty. If you were to go into Venusia on Thursday and speak with him before the vet..."

"Fine, don't worry. I'll do it."

Gallego would never have imagined that the foreman... But perhaps it was only a coincidence. Natividad had been talking about this insemination matter for days. But the way in which he had approached it this time could be interpreted as a favor to Macario. One thing was clear: he wanted to know whether or not he would be in Venusia on Thursday. All of a sudden he recalled that it was Natividad who had told him about the buried arms as if he were implicitly asking for his blessing, or at least for some sort of tacit assurance that he would not call the police. It was not too farfetched to assume that Natividad and Macario were in this together. The typesetter had grown up at Trebujar and spent considerable time with Natividad and Amparo's children.

Antonio Gallego left Trebujar right after lunch on Thursday.

He was hoping to get back that very night even though he had to talk with the administrator, run several errands and be at the Café Viena at seven. But, in case there was a delay and he didn't make it back until the next morning, he asked Gabriela not to wait up for him as she was in the habit of doing. And especially not to worry. He was convinced that nothing would happen to him. He was not involved in Macario's plans. He had known him all his life, Macario was the child of his nursemaid, no one could find anything suspicious in their relationship. It was a long way from there to participating in Macario's harebrained schemes. Besides, this would be it. He felt that he had amply returned the favor. He was going to tell Macario this very afternoon, as soon as he saw him. And if he did not show up, he would tell the go-between. Of course, there was no certainty that Macario was involved in conspiracies. Maybe he was trafficking in drugs, which would be even worse. The last thing he needed just now was to be dragged into illegal dealings. Now less than ever. Now that I have nothing to fear. I lead a retiring life, no one would associate me with any political organization after such a long time. No one, that is, except his own family or Corbalán. You're getting paranoid, he said to himself... Corbalán is in Europe, attending parties, courting all the Blancas that cross his path, working with the exiled Patiño to reinstate democracy to Itálica. No, I'm no longer a dangerous character. Besides, there's Gabriela. He feels very well-loved and his self-confidence is growing. He is happy, almost happy. When he writes, the ideas come with the ease of his younger years. Yes, this is a very good period for him.

First he took care of the matter of the insemination. "Natividad has gone mad," observed the administrator. "We had worked it all out and now he changes his mind. I'll give him a talking to on Saturday." Then he stopped by two bookstores. He bought sweets for his sister and a sapphire ring for Gabriela. It was an expensive but far from ostentatious gift that could scarcely be interpreted as an engagement ring, even though it certainly was. He would take her hand and slip it on claiming to have found it on the street, or saying that Macario's friends had paid him in goods.

He arrived at the cafe early despite the heavy traffic, worse than usual due to a strike of public transportation workers. Every privately owned vehicle seemed to be out on the streets and, even though there were not that many cars in Venusia altogether, the change was noticeable. Like the last time, he sat near the door and ordered a cognac. It was five to seven. He picked up a newspaper that had been left on a nearby table. As he was leafing through it someone greeted him from behind. He turned his head. He recognized the voice but not the face. This time the young man had his hair slicked down and a mustache; he wore no sunglasses and looked like a tango singer in the final stages of tuberculosis.

"You like to arrive first. Good strategy. That way, even if you have to wait, you can watch the other approach and get a chance to look him over."

"Wrong. I had five minutes to spare and the most comfortable way of spending them was in a chair. Why make you wait since I had agreed to come any way? I assume that Manzanas will show up soon, or will I be smoking with you again this time?"

The man smiled at the irony in Gallego's words. He seemed less nervous than the first time. He took out a pack of cigarettes and offered Antonio one.

"You must be curious to know why we asked you to come back."

"You bet. But let me warn you that this is it for me."

"It's impossible for the master to meet you here but you will see him today. They have asked me to take you there."

"Where?"

"Don't worry. You trust Macario, right?"

"Well, I've known him since we were children. But I have no intention of getting involved in dubious affairs. I'll let him know as soon as I see him."

"That's between the two of you. My job is to take you where they're waiting for us. We can leave whenever you're ready."

They stepped outside. A fine rain was falling. Tiny drops knitted short-lived lace mantillas on pedestrians, wove fleeting flower petals on vehicles, and scattered hundreds of blurry moons over the asphalt. The young man signaled him aboard his motorcycle and they sped off through the traffic. The noise of the motor made conversation between them difficult. They went north out of Venusia, on a back road. Behind them lay the suburban perimeter and the paved streets. The motorcycle stopped when they reached a cluster of buildings.

"You can get off. Macario will be here soon."

"What if he doesn't come?"

"I assure you he will be here immediately."

"All this time I have been thinking that I don't even know your name. That bothers me. If I ever think of you again I won't know what to call you."

"I, on the other hand, know that you used to be called Valentín, right?"

"Hmmm....and how do you know that?"

"It's part of my work, Señor Gallego. You can think of me as Andrés, or Sergio if you prefer. Good luck and thank you."

It was past eight already. The city was more than an hour away. The rain was coming down heavily now, and darkness was closing in. There was light on a window in the left wing of the seemingly abandoned building. Suddenly he made out Macario walking towards him. He had the collar of his sweater turned up around his ears and was wearing a plaid cap. The typesetter squeezed his hand and then, in a thoroughly unusual gesture, embraced him while thanking him.

"Before we go any further I want you to clarify all these puzzles for me. At the very least I'd like to know who I'm risking my neck for. It's only fair, don't you agree? And let me make it clear that I'm not coming back."

"As soon as we're over this hurdle I'll tell you everything. I promise. But I can't just now. It's actually to protect you, for your safety I mean. My truck is behind that house. Please come with me."

As he followed along Antonio Gallego was thinking that these people used up a lot of fuel. In his time conspiracies were done on foot.

"Are we going far?"

"No, no, it's right nearby. They sealed off my printing shop yesterday. They thought I was putting out subversive stuff."

"And it's true, of course."

"Yeah, but they didn't find any. I had already passed it on. Tomorrow we'll blanket Venusia with pamphlets. They'll be thrown from buses, from balconies... Personally, I think it's a waste of time. We need more violent action. If I were the one giving the orders..."

Antonio Gallego felt very ill at ease. He was itching to get it over with, see Manzanas, translate whatever it was, and be on his way.

"Here we are. Fortunately it's not raining anymore. Just in case, I have an umbrella here. Do you want it?"

"Do you think the time has now come to open it?"

Macario smiled conspiratorially. They were silent as they walked down a path leading to the stables. It smelled of hay, of manure, of damp earth. The stable door was padlocked. Macario took out a key from his pocket and opened it. They walked towards the back, stepping between two rows of cattle. Gallego was expecting Manzanas to materialize from behind a stack of hay since there was no other place for him to hide, unless he had disguised himself as a cow. Macario pushed two bales of straw aside from behind the mangers, cleared the floor of hay and dung, and opened a trap door that went down a spiral staircase.

"Please follow me."

He lit the way with a match so Gallego would not stumble. When they reached the bottom, the glare from a flashlight blinded them.

"It's us."

Gallego heard Macario's voice echo. The flashlight was no longer fixed on them.

"Not a very cozy place to welcome you, Señor Gallego."

Antonio had never heard that voice before and the words seemed insultingly mundane. The cellar was around fifteen square meters. A cot was on one corner next to a folding table, and across the room there were three chairs, a box of books, and a portable typewriter.

"I had you brought here so we could have some privacy. Do you like my hideaway? I can afford to show it to you since I'll go to a different one as soon as you leave. Don't be offended. I trust you. I know you were in jail and they couldn't get a word out of you. You're no informer."

"How do you know?"

"I also know that Corbalán accused you of doing precisely the opposite, and that you were expelled from the party because they thought you had ratted on Alberto Viertel. But Viertel was a double agent who had infiltrated the party ranks, and at some point the police feigned an arrest to get him away without raising suspicions. I know because I met him. He was a teacher like me. He worked for Luzón's secret police."

Even in the dim light one could almost see through the handkerchief that hid half of the teacher's face below the eyes. His features, coarse and vulgar as if chipped with a hatchet, stood out under the fabric. But what most impressed Gallego were his hands, rough and covered with poorly healed wounds, the hands of a sailor or a farm worker. Those hands belied the fact that Roberto Manzanas had spent more than twenty years of his life correcting spelling tests, or at the blackboard teaching the basics of arithmetic. Manzanas underlined everything he said with gestures. Often his open palms, clenched fists, or accusing fingers were more eloquent than his voice or his words. His short, thick frame and protruding belly seemed to disappear behind those large hands, so disproportionate that he could have used them as shields. He had better cover his hands instead of his face—Antonio Gallego was thinking—, they just give him away.

"I read your Goethe translations. For a while I was interested in German literature. My mother was from there and I speak the language. But Goethe is not my favorite. He berated the revolution every time he referred to it. Moreover, do you know what he thought of the common people, of the masses? That they would've been better off never having been born..."

"Excuse me, but Goethe was quoting Ariosto that time. You must say what I can do for you... If you speak German I can't see why you need my help...unless..."

Gallego did not finish the sentence. He was growing impatient. He could not understand why Manzanas was taking so long to tell him what this emergency was all about. He assumed that the purpose of this meeting was not to debate Goethe's political and literary views.

"I gather you want to get to the point, Señor Gallego. I speak with such few people, particularly as well-educated as you. I enjoyed your essay about Corbalán. He's a traitor. I know him well. I've been told that he's back in Itálica and the police are looking for him because of his involvement with Patiño."

"I can well imagine that you are eager for conversation but I don't believe this is either the time or the place to indulge. I am in a hurry. I must get back to Trebujar tonight. In other words..."

"I'll come right to the point. We need some information from you. We want to know the layout of the offices of *El Día*."

"I understand that *Radio Nacional* has moved its headquarters there now," replied Gallego.

"Yes. That's precisely why we need to find out every detail about the building."

Manzanas went to the cot and took some folded papers from under the thin mattress.

"This is the plan of the building. Look it over. Can you recall any other details? Was there a bunker in the cellar?"

"Yes."

"Please mark the doors. You used it as an escape once when police were after you. It leads to the sewers, if I'm not mistaken."

"That's correct. But how did you find out?"

"I've had access to confidential files. But none of us is a traitor, I guarantee that."

Gallego marked the entrance to the underground chamber.

"Thank you. Now all you have to do is translate the final communiqué," he said holding out a sealed envelope for him to open. "Please read it out loud."

Gallego complied.

148

"*Die Ladung ist vorbereitet. Die Wetteraussichten sind günstig.*" He proceeded to translate what he had just read. "The shipment is ready. The weather forecast is good."

"Please, would you type a reply in German? Write: Everything is prepared."

Gallego obeyed. Without sitting down he keyed in *alles ist fertig.* When he had finished he walked toward the staircase in order to leave. Macario followed him.

"Am I free to go now?"

"Yes, of course. We won't be bothering you again. Thank you very much."

Manzanas shook his hand. He squeezed it as hard as a heavyweight champion, celebrating with his manager after winning the world title in the last round.

X

First there was a convulsive noise, brakes skidding on the driveway gravel. Next, the clanging of the gate as it was forced open, together with the dogs' barking into the night. Then came the footsteps, metal-ribbed boots that hammered their way across the tiles. Unfamiliar voices yelling his name as the lights of the ground floor rooms go on. Unfamiliar voices seeking him out, over that of the foreman who repeats that he is not here, that he left Trebujar that afternoon and won't be back for a week. Unfamiliar voices demanding that the dogs be restrained, lest they be forced to practice marksmanship on them, and ordering that the doors be opened because they have a search order and a warrant for the owner's arrest. But, in his absence, they have no objection to talking with his sister or his cousin, or with both, in an appropriate place of course, not here of course, but down the road at the regional headquarters, at Olimpia Military Barracks. It's just routine questioning but it must be done on official premises—they have nothing to do with death squads, or with gangs that kidnap and torture—that way citizens can be assured of the full exercise of their legal rights. They assume that Doña Constanza Gallego will be free to return to Trebujar the next day, once she has given her testimony before the official in charge of the case.

"You're mistaken, Natividad, I am here. I postponed the trip until tomorrow. Please state what urgent business brings you here to wake us at this hour."

He had heard every noise, the abrupt braking of the jeep, the loud slamming of the doors, the struggle with the gate, the dogs' insistent barking, their jeering voices asking for him, sparring with the foreman's own, and the excuses: "The master is not in." It was true, he was not there, he was elsewhere, in another world. He was traversing newly discovered waters, exploring them night after night.

"Thank you, Natividad. You can go back to bed. What can I do for you..."

He is followed by the howling of the dogs and the forceful steps. Once again the noise of the gate and its metallic grating, the roar of the engine, the tires spitting gravel as if looking for smoother surfaces under the sharp edges of the stones.

Many hours later, when he wakes up in a huge hall surrounded by strangers, he continues to hear those sounds over a background of howling dogs while, with stupefied eyes, he watches the scene in disbelief. Faces, old ones, young ones, faces of children, and men, and women, a desolate throng packed tightly together, heaped on a floor damp and slimy with the human waste oozing from each body, from every pore of every body, like in a pigsty, together like pigs waiting to go to market, waiting to be weighed and whipped into a truck that will take them to the slaughterhouse. Then they will be herded into a steril-ized hall, the death chamber where veterinarians will ex-amine them carefully prior to vivisecting them. Worse than a pigsty. I can't hear their final grunts but instead I listen to screams, whimpers, moans. Suddenly a military march is heard over the din, drowning it out with clash-ing cymbals, blaring trumpets, rolling drums. The re-gional commander has arrived—explains an old man lying by his side—that's the way they greet him every morning. The same way, every morning. But he asks nothing, says nothing. He does not dare. He notices his shirt sticking to his back. It's agonizingly hot and muggy, and a noxious stench hangs in the air. No, that's really the aroma of fresh violets. He buries his face in the volup-tuous chestnut-colored mane, he brings to his mouth the warm hands that reach out to him in the darkness, with his tongue he traces new itineraries on the cherished skin. He sees only her eyes, like aquamarines, hears no voices other than hers, close, so close; there are no moans, no cries but hers at the height of lovemaking. Everything else is a nightmare. He is merely dreaming that scene, he is watching it in a film about torture, a documentary sponsored by an international Jewish organization to show the world the horror of the Nazi extermination camps. Or perhaps he is just remembering another time, another jail. No. There come the sounds again, the shrill screeching of the brakes, the clicking of boots against the tiles, against his head, as if everything is happening inside his mind. The sentries are watching. Some guards aim the black mouths of their rifles, others hit the prisoners with the butts to force them to move, to make them crawl towards a door where they await their turn to go who knows where, summoned by who knows whom.

I don't want to see worms slithering down cheeks, nor hear the ever higher howling of dogs, an omen of death, spreading like a condor's wings. They're calling for me. They're yelling my name. Where from? They order me to get up and come forward among thousands of heads, hands, legs, thousands of people who are also waiting. It's all right to step on them. Their limbs are lifeless, their flesh rotted, they no longer feel pain. They order me to hurry, hurry, faster, up to the armored door, to ignore the groans, the sobs, the death-rattle of the dying. I haven't done anything. A brief and routine questioning. I might be an alcoholic in the midst of delirium tremens, surrounded by ghosts waiting to pounce. Like Olvido playfully covered with a sheet in the hallway when I refused to eat my soup and was the brattiest one of the Señora's children. "You little devil with a snail on your forehead. Holy Mother, whatever will become of you? If you don't eat you won't grow. You'll stay a weakling, a little nothing, a Tom Thumb, a midget who will have to earn his keep in fairs, wandering from one place to another. What a shame for your poor parents! Come, have another spoonful. See, that's a good boy who finishes his soup... and he'll grow tall and strong like men." As he gets deeper into the golden woods of his childhood birds of tenderness fly through the blue sky.

"Antonio Gallego Cárdenas. Is that you?"

It's a disembodied voice that chides him, coming out of nowhere. There is no one at the end of the hall which is flanked by armored doors. The eyes of death are looking at him through the keyholes.

"Yes it is. Who wants to know?"

He is pushed into the darkness. He can barely breathe in the empty room. He is being suffocated by carbon monoxide and anguish. He lowers his head and writhes. There are no windows. They bolted the door behind him. There is no escape. All at once the glare, a scorching floodlight that sets his eyes on fire. His eyes become a void, the sockets burn, the eyelids turn to ashes. He cannot open them. He cannot move. He tries to concentrate on his breathing. Has he gotten used to the carbon monoxide? He focuses exclusively on the rhythm of his lungs. Inhale, exhale, as if his life depended on keeping track of the game his lungs are playing with the air. With the gas? He can't open his eyes. The pain will not let him, the pain flowing down his cheeks. Even with his eyes closed he perceives the light dimming slightly. It is not so powerful anymore. Has his skin adjusted or is it losing its sensitivity? He uses his hand as a shield. Little by little, as if following a doctor's instructions, he begins to lift his eyelids. Now there is a diffuse light in which he can make out shapes, objects. A table, two chairs, a file cabinet. He sits down and leans back only to be jolted by an electric shock. He bleats like a sheep flung down a gorge. The door opens.

He feels his limbs come back to life. He moves his legs, clenches his fists, opens them again.

There is an army uniform with a colonel's rank on the other side of the table. His words maim. "We must have these appliances repaired. They go off on their own, without any warning. I hope you will understand." A cynical sneer is permanently etched on his features.

"We found weapons on your property. Were you aware of that? They were buried. That carries a heavy sentence. Weapons for the guerrillas, for those damned terrorists who want to destroy Itálica, who have sold out to the Communist International. They were manufactured in the Soviet Union. What groups do you belong to? Do you know any of the members of Red Dawn? Who belongs to AVE? Do you know that in addition to being terrorists they're also cocaine dealers? Have you met Manzanas? What's your relation with Macario? Do you know that your cousin has disappeared from Calipso? That your uncle is under arrest for subversive activities? Have you any notion of what will happen to you if you don't cooperate, if you don't tell us the truth? We've been keeping close tabs on you, each one of your comings and goings is recorded. We know your life inside out... Your correspondence with the Patiño government, your opposition to Luzón... your Marxist leanings of long standing. You won't be needing a lawyer... It's no use. Lawyers can't help you anymore. You'd better cooperate. Not only for your sake but for your family's. Those two women depend on you. Better tell us everything. Get ready to confess. Be prepared to tell us everything you know or you'll regret it. Take this as friendly advice. Notice how cordially I'm explaining your options. I abhor welts and bruises, blows that disfigure a face, electric shocks to your genitals, the rack, the prod, and all the other instruments that we have to resort to when someone refuses to come clean. Well, it's up to you. We're talking about your future, your personal well-being. You have nothing to say? Impossible. Nothing to tell us? How can that be? You, the son of a candidate of the Radical Party? A member, or rather ex-member, of the Communist Party? A friend of Macario? Natividad's boss? Natividad tried to protect you, but he'll never do that again. Want to know why? Simple. The person who was interrogating him got kind of nervous and cut off his tongue... Natividad can be very defiant. Without his tongue he won't be able to tell us any names, that's true, but he'll also never speak again. Would you like to see him? Do you want proof that I'm not lying, that I'm an honorable man, that I do this type of work out of deep conviction and love for my country, out of absolute hatred for those who want to tear it apart? Come with me, it's not far, just two doors down at the infirmary."

He sees Natividad lying in a corner, barely conscious, with a purplish mass for lips, twitching in the throes of death.

XI

Only a wall. No other horizon. A wall. An uneven surface without openings, without cracks to let in a ray of light, a breath of air. A peeling yet solid wall. Or perhaps not. A hole, a pit, a sewer. Toads croaking, trails of slugs. Bubbling, putrid ponds. A thick magma, a rotten brew of feces, of dead creatures, of stagnant waters, of mutilated bodies. A feast for vultures and other birds of prey. A route for ants in perfect file, in mourning, like mute weepers following a funeral, their heads held low, awaiting their booty. Don't run away soul-butterfly because you will be eaten by insects and you will reincarnate in your own dead body forever. Forever. Wait. Take shelter under the blanket of insects, get ready to hum along during the ceremony. As soon as the crows get here the prayer for the dead and the requiem mass can begin. May he never rest in peace, may eternal hatred be with him forever and ever. May an iron fist strike his gut, may the hand that wields knives, picks, pliers, hammers, never allow him to rest under the earth. Let scalpels and poisoned daggers drill into him over and over again.

"If you don't tell me Macario's hiding place you'll never get out of here. Never, never, never."

Only time ahead of you. The wall, the sewer your one horizon, the only landscape. Time behind you, on your back like a load; memory reaching for life. The fields of Trebujar, reds, ochres, licked by the shimmering light of dusk—maybe right now, maybe five hours ago—and now it is dark and the oxen are pulling carriages of stars. The crickets are singing. Sheep bleat. Cows bellow in the stables, impatient for the moment when the doors will fling open and shepherds and cowhands will take them out to pasture. Tender sprigs of grass, thin new shoots, luscious honeysuckle to be bitten off and chewed eagerly and gladly. What month is this? Is it rainy August or misty July when the fog hovers around the peaks and covers the hills with robes of silk? Are the leaves falling yet? Or is it torrid December, the heat bursting forth in the humming of bees, the rustle of insects by the enchanted pond, the piercing midday torch finishing off the frail wildflowers, enflaming the branches of the myrrh tree like lightning bolts? Sparkling clearings that he will never see again and that he now conjures up grabbing at the edges of memories, trying to keep them alive in his mind. Where lies summer? In what direction? He does not wonder about past summers—perhaps still lingering on his skin—but about the ones he will miss. And he recalls the cruelest of months blooming in an inhospitable but still beautiful world, there beyond the walls and sewers, far from here, away from this prison, from the Xiqué Penal Colony where time is not measured in hours, nor its passing in faces in the mirrors. Time advancing, time without light or darkness, time nonexistent outside his own pulse, the beating of his heart, its rhythmic contracting and expanding. Through dead veins the heart pumps a red watery liquid, the blood of dead oxen, of dead calves, of dead lambs, all killed by the storm. How many months? How many years? How many decades? Calendar leaves fall haphazardly. Is this August? December? December is the hottest month, when humidity makes the walls sweat and garbage floats in puddles. It's always the same time, time to wait, time for nothing. The hour of death. The hour of suffering. The hour to walk out to the courtyard never to return. The hour of failure. The hour of silence broken by moans, by executioners' shots, never by words. No one talks, no one chats. Inquiries are like iron hooks the shape of question marks, like the spurs of fighting cocks with sharp-edged combs. Answers are given with cutting, poisoned words when possible, or with others drenched in fear and revulsion. Enough. Enough. Enough. Used-up words, words appropriated by street hawkers to sell their wares, words spit out by gamblers. Lost words, neither heard nor spoken, words scratched on walls over and against other older words. «And light cut through the darkness and, against the word, the world continued spinning around the core of the word unsaid.»

Words resonate in the cell. A name. Blanca's name that saved him then, in that other jail, the name-amulet that protected him against those other guards; or Gabriela's, firestone for his nights, flaming stone in the branches of his veins in a ritual as futile as it is devastating. Incriminating words, the names of Macario and Natividad, the names that jump out at him from the wall. He is afraid he will scream for help in his dreams, he will beg for forgiveness even though he's innocent, only to get out of that place, away from that nightmare. But it is the other words that he attempts to say. My country, what did I do to you? Where can I find the word? Where is it echoing? In what place? In which direction? Where can it be heard? Gabriela. Gabriela, are you listening? Can you hear me cry out your name? Does my voice reach your ears? The word resonates along the roads, in the darkness, during the day as well as at night. This is not the right place, nor the proper time. There are no mirrors and I cannot see the shape of my lips as I form those names that I so love, the names that used to dispel the darkness but that have been slowly emptied of their magic, like shells that hold the murmur of a false sea. Always a murmur. Only a murmur. The breaking of the waves in this empty silence, the silence of the executioners, the silence of the closed eyes of the dead that are filing past, that attack from behind. Murmur of waves in my ear, of dead waves in a dead sea, saying nothing to the hot sand, the silence of a desert night. The lilacs are probably blooming already, and the neon lights must have come on in Venusia and Calipso. There are cinemas showing films, and people coming out of restaurants before curfew. There are patrols along the avenues, and kidnappings, and stray bullets that may kill or wound. In spite of this public terror, it is nice to go for a stroll, even a quick one, even if just to get to a specific place from which you can reach home before doors are shut and metal grates let down. To look out the window toward the docks of Calipso and notice the movement of merchant ships in the harbor, and further out the steamers floating like seagulls in the immense ocean. To ponder which cognac to order, shall it be the expensive French one, so smooth and aromatic, carrying a double luxury tax? To smell the flowers at the center of a table exquisitely set with linen tablecloth and napkins, offering delicacies new to the palate. To listen to Bach, or Vivaldi, or Wagner, exultant, magnificent with rolling drums and horns, a cascade of melodious metals and a hurricane of musical winds. Isolde's voice draped in mourning, skimming a tranquil lake like Lohengrin. The sounds of the music that I listened to for so long, chords and notes created by violins, allegro con brio, as the piano takes up the orchestra's theme, a cadence that thins until it's almost inaudible only to climb to the sharpest note. Would he recognize Bach or Beethoven or Mozart after listening to so much silence, so much discordant din? The blasts of shots, of excavating machines, the groans of torture chambers in the hours of darkness. The clatter of footsteps at the end of the hall, of footsteps coming near. The clanging of dishes and pots in the patio when they line us up to feed us, fast, faster, no time to talk, to exchange words of warning or of hope.

"Well, you've had time to reflect. What do you think about the commander's proposal?"

He could never have anticipated it, even though his ghost was at hand even in the clearest of nights, in the most glorious of days, in the sweetest of dawns, in the softest of dusks. He never would have thought about such a possibility to recover the words and, later, even his freedom. Without ceasing to be himself he has to become another. He has to transform himself. He has to put on a disguise, like Goethe: the clothes of a humble student, a dressed-up country boy. To avert Lucinda's curse from Friederike's lips. A disguise that is more than clothes, more than gestures. A disguise made up mainly of words, continuing that which is already written, in a similar style, with identical patterns, with the same intentions, so that coherence will not be jeopardized, so that it will seem the product of one mind, written by the very same hand.

The time is now. The time when all the clocks coincide, when all the bells ring in unison. Perhaps his entire life has been nothing but a preparation for this chance event.

He is holding a notebook in his hands. One hundred sheets of lined paper. One hundred sheets that he must return, written, each one of them. One hundred sheets to continue *Relay*, a novel that was already begun on those sheets, its first words petrified, nailed, chiseled onto that notebook. Words to which only he can give wings, which only he can launch into flight, if he can manage to break the spell, to liberate them from their shackles, their chains, their handcuffs. He must free them from all prisons, give them light from eyes other than the guards' or his own, exhausted by staring so long at the same wall, the same swampy opening to the sewer.

XII

The years pass. They pass and take with them a face. A face transformed by scalpels that copy a certain turn of the lips, another face's features, always in search of the image on the photograph. And the miracle begins to seem possible. Soon they will be able to show the world the prisoner that many governments have interceded for, the name repeated on telegrams, the name written on posters with capital letters: CORBALÁN.

The years pass and take with them a face. His hair has turned gray, he holds a pencil in his hand, and a notebook with exactly one hundred pages. Not one less. The picture appears in all the newspapers. Corbalán is alive. He has cleverly managed to sneak out of prison fragments of what he is writing, on cigarette paper. They provide minimal but encouraging evidence. Prison has not completely destroyed him, at least he does not seem as badly affected as was feared. Foreign newspapers rejoice at the news. In Itálica itself some opposition circles acknowledge it, not without skepticism. Nevertheless no one can stretch the imagination enough to guess that it is nothing but a skillfully prepared mirage. That behind every written word, every single letter, stand the most ruthless of guards. No one suspects that someone else is completing Corbalán's draft; someone who has taken his name, who has exchanged his life for another's, traded his past for an uncertain future hoping only to escape the darkness and return to the light. His purpose is to recover in body and soul, to reclaim his hopes and personality, and to secure some kind of place in the history of literature.

He must memorize his habits, replicate his gestures, mimic his character, imitate his behavior in every respect. He's lucky to have known him since adolescence, to have shared some experiences—the love for Blanca among them—, to have completed such an exhaustive analysis of *Senseless Days*, to have done time at the Xiqué prison while he was there too, feeling caught in his reflection. He is like a failed actor who doubles for the star in dangerous scenes, eager to assume his role, until by sheer force of repetition even the fans confuse them and invite him to fancy parties at the mansions of millionaires. But in the end he gives himself away because the double, instead of accepting the flattery in stride, feels the need to return it in kind. He underlines the harshness of the face, the peacock's well-hidden pride, the crow-like predatory instincts.

He is an artist, a creator. He has the talent to conceive a whole new world, to beget other beings and then dispose of them if he so chooses. He has the power to move entire armies across the plains, to defy the dangers of the deep sea in a fragile kayak, or to lead a luxury liner full of mindless passengers through a violent storm where they will end their lives in shark-infested waters. He can bring on laughter or tears, stop time to eternalize a moment, that moment where the past is held and preserved.

But he knows better than most those sorrowful hours, the small sleepless hours of interminable vigil at the desk, obsessed—like Captain Ahab with his adversary—with the void, the whiteness that at once attracts and repels. A blank page that he attempts to fill with the sharp tip of his feather pen or with the tiny mechanical tongues of the typewriter, lovingly or desperately beating back the void.

No. This is not what he wants to write. These are not the exact words, nor those either. All-purpose words, words like docile farm chickens, fodder-fed in clean coops with piped-in music. He wants words that will shake the earth as well as the life of whoever reads them, that will pierce the skin and touch the soul. Words like those used in creating Werther, Faust, Madame Bovary, or Marcel.

Goethe stated that when one knows the classics, when one is familiar with all that has been written, one does not feel compelled to add anything. He believes this too. It is the truth. Yet he himself will write for the sake of survival. He has been ordered to do it: "Continue what he started. Finish it." Did he not assert that *Senseless Days* was plagiarized? That the idea was his own, that he had written about a hundred pages on that theme with a similar plot? Perhaps there is a strange force that keeps bringing them together just as it pushes them apart, as if they had been but one person in another life, one of those androgynous beings who challenged the gods and were split in half. So why not take up *Relay*? No one will be able to tell that someone else wrote more than half, that it beats to a different drummer, just as no one noticed that *Senseless Days* was the continuation of something, of a text found in a suitcase. He writes because he wants to go out into the streets and see people again, even if from within someone else's skin, even if under another's name. Afterwards, once he has served his purpose, he will go back to Trebujar, to the red earth, to the brown fields, to Gabriela if she is still alive, if she can still bring herself to open the door and let him in after such a long time. He writes guided by the obsession of seeing what the years have done to the faces he loves, by the desire that they might still be alive. That's why he agreed. This is his only chance to get out of here, otherwise he will continue to rot forever. No one writes his name on a placard, no diplomats demand his freedom. He is just another faceless prisoner. Whenever they tire of seeing him they will just shove him into a common grave and neither Gabriela nor Constanza will even be given the opportunity to identify his remains.

He writes the final chapters. He is almost finished. He has been told that as soon as he is done he will be able to leave Catantú, the minimum security prison where he was sent after Corbalán died for lack of proper medical attention. An unforgivable mistake, letting Corbalán go like that just when the eyes of the world were fixed on the famous prisoner of Xiqué. How could they justify his passing if, under pressure from international organizations, they had agreed to set him free unharmed? Gallego can be useful. They are familiar with the ins and outs of his relation with Corbalán. They probably intuit that his need for revenge was not satisfied by the blow that knocked out Corbalán's front teeth. Here is another chance that he must not fail to exploit. They will release him from Catantú but he must carry on the farce a while longer. Then, once his mission is accomplished, he can go back to being Gallego. He is sworn to forget the whole thing, to forever suppress that he became Corbalán. One word out of him, the slightest suspicious move, and he will be wasted at once.

He undergoes rigorous training. He absorbs Corbalán's habits, his gestures, his favorite books and meals. He has practically memorized his œuvre, as if he himself had written it. He reproduces his handwriting as closely as possible, studies his repertoire of dedications, practices his way of sitting, of kissing ladies' hands the way he saw him do it during their acquaintance in Calipso, the way the experts coach him. He gradually blends his ways with Corbalán's, subordinating his own behavior patterns. He emphasizes the harshness, the aggression, the sarcastic magnanimity, the carefully studied eloquence sprinkled with pious rhetoric. He follows instructions closely, and is actually rather pleased with the results. His revenge will be all the sweeter for making Corbalán play the traitor, one who has turned suspiciously moderate. Naturally, he does not see eye to eye with the government which incarcerated him, but the years spent first in a camp near

Calipso and later in Xiqué, have made him more cautious, less rash. He has had plenty of time to reflect on the country's situation. He has been thrown together with revolutionaries whose ideas he does not share, he has witnessed the country's undeclared civil war. Needless to say he still condemns totalitarianism in any shape or form, as well as all dictatorships. But he has outgrown the radical Marxism of his youth. He is now a liberal who admits that, even though Cardona's government has made its share of mistakes, the country needed a sharp turn, a strong hand to set its new course. And he states it plainly, despite his friendship with Patiño, who was so good to him. And he goes on about national reconciliation, about tolerance and forbearance. These are the three basic points, now that Cardona is talking about purging his cabinet of the most radical ministers and forming a new one to include representatives of moderate groups which have been active in the ranks of the opposition up to now.

XIII

He does not sleep despite the tranquilizers. He lies awake, waiting for the new day although there is still no trace of dawn in the darkness. These are his last hours at Catantú. Tomorrow a plane will take him to New York, together with a secretary and a bodyguard, paid by the government, who will make sure that he sticks to the script and makes no mistakes. The grand performance is about to begin: in the morning, at the airport, before at least one hundred journalists, international observers, members of Amnesty International, and delegates from the Red Cross, Pablo Corbalán will answer a few questions, safely hiding Antonio Gallego in the deepest recesses of his soul. He will dodge the flashbulbs although their intermittent flames do not compare to search lights, or to the continuous and blinding intensity that burned his eyelids that first time he was questioned at Olimpia Military Barracks. But since his eyes will never forget that scorching glare, he will request that they stop taking pictures, that they save their flashbulbs, that they forego the welcoming fireworks. He is alive and only two hours away from freedom.

He will be deeply moved for someone else's sake, before the foreign correspondents who will observe him respectfully, who will approach him ready to take down his first statements after his release from captivity. He will express his profound gratitude for their interest, he will allow himself to be embraced. And, to end the brief press conference that the likes of actors, athletes, or politicians merit, he will flash them his flawless smile. He will show his perfect teeth that never required a visit to the dentist; teeth miraculously saved from the raging fist of jealous colleagues hungry for recognition. He will bid them farewell with a raised hand while the other will signal victory with trembling fingers, for the secret satisfaction of other fingers that would doubtlessly scratch the air in a similar gesture.

He feels restless and uneasy in this vigil, his pulse is racing. He wonders how he will react the first time he grants an interview. No matter that he can predict exactly how Corbalán would answer after studying so many of his responses, he is still anxious. He would prefer to assert what he, Antonio Gallego, feels about literature, about the world, about politics, about his country. He worries that the truth, which he must for the moment conceal, will slip out. He must save the real answers for later, after Corbalán vanishes and Gallego is once more in control. He fears—although he denies it to himself—that someone might challenge his identity, not accept him as who he says he is. Someone like Blanca, for instance. What would happen if he stumbled into Blanca? Probably nothing after all these years since, actually, he and Corbalán spent about the same time in jail. He is fortunate that Corbalán never married or had children, at least legitimate ones. That keeps him from having to play a melodramatic scene that he is not at all certain he could pull off persuasively. He has reached an agreement with them, Comandante García and his thugs. He will try to keep it low key. He will avoid large receptions, meetings with other Italicans, television appearances. Any interviews will be monitored by the secretary and the bodyguard who will stick to the same line: Corbalán is very tired and quite weak. Sometimes he has lapses of memory. He is under doctors' care.

He tries not to panic. Why now that it's almost over, now that he has accepted a different name which will free him from the horror, from the infinite revulsion, from the endless pain? Now that death no longer acts the broody hen, waiting around for him to hatch. He is afraid that he will be recognized when his picture comes out in tomorrow's newspapers, as soon as the plane leaves the country. His mission has been conscientiously planned. Two public appearances in Spain, plus a press conference. Altogether less than two weeks. And then back to anonymity and unconditional freedom. They have shown him his passport with the name of Antonio Gallego Cárdenas, occupation: landowner. A passport he can use to return to Itálica whenever he wishes, as soon as he reads his speech at the Peace Conference which will begin eight days from now in Madrid. The speech, needless to say, has been prepared for him. He does not have to attend many sessions or even stay until the end of the conference. He is supposed to read and leave under the pretext of his precarious health. Corbalán will disappear mysteriously so that Antonio Gallego can come back to life. If everything goes well, of course, if he does not blunder. And that is entirely up to him. In a few months he will be able to make his way back to Trebujar. Beforehand he must undergo some more surgery. But Gallego does not believe them. If he agreed to the fraud it's only because he has no option. He must exercise extreme caution, particularly when he is abroad. He must outsmart his companions, take the initiative in disposing of Corbalán and restoring his true identity before his life is in grave peril. He must leave traces, establish an alibi to prove that he is Antonio Gallego and has been forced to stand in for Corbalán. He must persuade everyone that he did it because it was his only opportunity to denounce the horrors, the torture, the crimes that his people have endured. He will speak of his own ordeal. He will tell the whole truth. He will refer to his hatred for Corbalán, which has by now waned. No, he won't play along to the end. He will ask for political asylum as soon as he gets to Madrid. Or rather, why not try it immediately at Kennedy Airport? No, perhaps it's best not to rush. He knows that there will be journalists there to meet him, as well as Italican exiles to whom he has been forbidden to talk. He also expects the president of PEN Club International to be there. Maybe he can find a moment alone with him to tell him everything. Or at least give him some clues. Somehow he must leave traces of his real identity. He is the author of *Relay*, his masterpiece, the work that he prefers to *Senseless Days* even though the latter made him famous. Maybe they won't keep him under such strict surveillance and possibly he might even walk to the headquarters of some international organization and break open the case. Will they believe him? Or will they think that he, Corbalán, has gone insane as a result of the ordeal and suggest that he be committed?

He keeps watch through a night of insomnia, his eyelids propped open by fear and immune to the effects of sleep-inducing drugs. He battles the frightened little man, bound hand and foot, that weeps deep down inside him.

EPILOGUE

Teresa Mascaró (Olot, Gerona, 1953) vanished from Venusia in January, 1979. For almost eight years her parents and I, who felt responsible for what had happened, tried every possible way to find her, with no results. The attempts of both her Italican friends and the members of Amnesty International in charge of her case, met with a similar fate.

Now after the fall of Cardona (March, 1987), and thanks to a report drafted by an investigating committee appointed by the new democratic government, we have found out that Teresa died on January 15, 1979. She perished in a fire that destroyed the manor at Trebujar inhabited by Constanza Gallego and her cousin Gabriela Orbajosa, also victims of the tragedy. The fire is believed to have been started by an arsonist.

Nothing, then, stands in the way of the publication of the manuscript that Teresa had smuggled out of the country and delivered to me. Unfortunately, it can no longer be of any good to her. I have also included some fragments of Teresa's journal that refer to Corbalán-Gallego, made available by her parents, as well as the six letters that she wrote to me from Itálica.

My purpose is twofold. First, I would like in this manner to remember Teresa, since each time we think of her in a way we bring her back to life. Secondly, I hope that these pages will persuade the police to take seriously the hypothesis that it is not Corbalán who is buried in the cemetery at Cerdanyola. I am certain that Antonio Gallego's perfect teeth will provide him the last laugh over his nemesis. From the Barrière Clinic in Paris I was able to obtain some dental X-rays belonging to Pablo

Corbalán which show two broken teeth that the eminent dentist rebuilt to perfection.

Celia Bestard

Catalan Studies
Translations and Criticism

The primary goal of this series of translations and scholarly books is to disseminate Catalan culture more widely in the English-speaking academic community. Preference is given to English-language translations and academic criticism, but manuscripts in Spanish or Catalan are also considered, as are studies addressing other aspects of Catalan culture and civilization. The series is co-sponsored by two institutions: the Center for Catalan Studies at The Catholic University of America, and the Paulí Bellet Foundation, both in Washington, DC. Authors may send queries to:

Dr. Josep M. Solà-Solé, General Editor
Center for Catalan Studies
Department of Modern Languages
The Catholic University of America
Washington, DC 20064

DATE DUE